Outdoor Living Skills Program Manual:

An Environmentally Friendly Guide

Outdoor Living Skills Program Manual:

An Environmentally Friendly Guide

Catherine M. Scheder

American Camping Association®

Copyright © 2002 by American Camping Association, Inc.

Printed in the United States of America

All rights reserved. No part of this book may be reproduced or transmitted in any form or by any means, electronic or mechanical, including photocopying, recording, or any information storage retrieval system, without permission in writing from the publisher.

Cover: ACA file photos; design of cover and text by Hura Design, Inc.

Text illustrations by Todd Criswell, Jean Hura, and courtesy of Girl Scouts of the USA from *Outdoor Education in Girl Scouting* and Camp Fire USA from *The Outdoor Book*.

All product and company names mentioned herein are the trademarks of their respective owners.

American Camping Association, Inc.
5000 State Road 67 North
Martinsville, IN 46151-7902
765-342-8456 national office
800-428-2267 bookstore
765-349-6357 fax
bookstore@ACAcamps.org e-mail
www.ACAcamps.org Web site

An updated version of Phyllis M. Ford's, *Take a New Bearing*, revised by Catherine M. Scheder.

Scheder, Catherine M. 1969-

ISBN 0-87603-175-0

A CIP catalog record for this book can be obtained from the Library of Congress.

Dedication

To Ann and Wendall
for having a dream
and leaving a legacy

Acknowledgments

Many thanks go to Phyllis Ford. Her original book, *Take a New Bearing*, has provided literally thousands of people with a basis from which to learn outdoor living skills. This solid foundation of work made this revision possible. Thanks also go to Dr. Sandra Hupp, Rhonda Mickelson, and Dr. Rita Yerkes for taking the time to review the content of this book and to make recommendations for improvements. I thank Connie Coutellier for her guidance and assistance in this process. I thank my parents, James and Carol Scheder, for instilling in me a love and respect for the natural world and my brothers, David, John, Greg, and Don, for letting their little sister join them in their outdoor adventures. And finally, for all who participate in outdoor experiences, may you continue to enjoy the great outdoors and promote and preserve it for future generations.

Table of Contents

Outdoor Living Skills

Part of Our Heritage

Since the dawn of time, people have explored the natural world. From early hunters and gatherers whose only means of survival was to adapt to living in an outdoor environment to today's outdoor enthusiasts who do it to learn and live and be one with nature, outdoor living skills are a part of our heritage as members of this living planet. Living outdoors brings us back to our roots and draws us closer to nature. Our curiosity for the natural world and our love for the outdoors have led us to learn skills that help us live outdoors comfortably and with minimal impact on the natural world.

History of Outdoor Living Skills in Camping

Gunnery Camp — ACA Historical File

The year 1861 marked the beginning of organized camping with the implementation of the Gunnery Camp in Washington, CT. Fred and Annabel Gunn took boys from their school, into the wilderness where they hiked, set up their camp, and spent two weeks boating, fishing, and trapping. Since that time, overnights, cookouts, and specific skills related to living in the outdoors have traditionally been a part of the camp experience.

Who Teaches Outdoor Living Skills?

Besides the American Camping Association (ACA), many summer camps and environmental education programs, colleges and universities and other programs such as the National Outdoor Leadership School (NOLS), Outward Bound, and Becoming an Outdoors-Woman teach outdoor living skills. Many youth and family-oriented programs such as Girl Scouts of the USA, Boy Scouts of America, YMCA, Boys and Girls Clubs, Camp Fire USA, 4-H, and religious organizations incorporate outdoor living skills into their programs. Whoever is conducting the program in outdoor living skills, the intended outcome is the same...for participants to walk away with a greater understanding and confidence in how to live comfortably in an outdoor environment and how to preserve it for future generations.

Outdoor Living Skills Program Manual: An Environmentally Friendly Guide

Recognizing the need for an organized program to teach outdoor living skills, ACA developed instructional material to assist in this process. Originally named Camp Crafters, the current Outdoor Living Skills (OLS) program provides participants with skills needed to explore the natural world while preserving it for future generations. Wherever we travel, whether through a national forest or a city park, on a short hike or a week-long backpacking adventure, we make choices, both positive and negative, that have an impact on our environment. OLS teaches participants environmental awareness, forges environmental ethics, and promotes environmental responsibility while learning skills to live comfortably in an outdoor environment.

The *Outdoor Living Skills Program Manual: An Environmentally Friendly Guide* is your compass for navigating through the ACA's Outdoor Living Skills program. The OLS program is designed to teach youth and adults the outdoor skills needed for a meaningful outdoor experience with little or no impact on the environment. The program is composed of five levels (earth, sun, water, weather, and stars). Each level teaches skills in

- map and compass reading,

- trip preparation and planning,

- food preparation and storage,

- knot tying,

- first aid and safety,

- environmental hazards,

- basic ecology,

- minimum-impact camping,

- outdoor hazards, and

- weather.

Each level is designed with the skill of the participant in mind. For example, Level I-Earth is for those with little or no outdoor experience and Level V-Stars allows participants to plan and lead an outdoor trip. The program is one of progression where participants can move at their own pace. There are no age requirements, and children as young as five or six can find success in Level I. Many of the skills required for each level can be done in conjunction with one another. Planning and taking a day hike, for example, are two skills that can be done in one time frame. With diligence and determination, each level can be completed in approximately one week. The advanced levels, IV-Weather and V-Stars, may take a little more time to complete because participants are challenged to complete more difficult and intricate skills.

Materials

A variety of materials that support the OLS program are available. In conjunction with this book, the OLS program uses the OLS Program Leaders field guides. Upon the completion of each level, participants can receive brightly colored patches to recognize their efforts and accomplishments. All materials are available from the ACA Bookstore.

Training

There are a variety of ways to implement the OLS program within your camp or organization. ACA has training opportunities available in most regions throughout the country for Program Leaders, Instructors, and Trainers. Training is offered by local offices of the American Camping Association and by other youth-serving organizations. Updates for all levels of training can be done online through ACA's online courses. Books and materials can also be purchased through the ACA Bookstore. To schedule a course, please contact your section education chair, an OLS instructor or trainer in your area, or the ACA National Office. All information can be found at www.acacamps.org/education/ols.htm or by contacting the American Camping Association for more information.

American Camping Association
5000 State Road 67 North
Martinsville, IN 46151-7902
800-428-CAMP (2267) ACA Bookstore
765-342-8456 American Camping Association
www.ACAcamps.org

Getting Started

ACA File Photo

By choosing to be a leader in the Outdoor Living Skills program, you have already taken a huge step in helping others enjoy their surroundings while protecting the environment. This book has been written to help you teach the skills necessary for having a positive, comfortable experience in the outdoors. You'll learn outdoor living skills that keep people safe, comfortable, and happy in an environment that is only temporarily their home. You'll also learn minimum-impact camping skills that help people leave the outdoors just the way they found it or better.

Although there are many individual skills, this book is also about sharing the outdoor experiences in a group. Outdoor activities in this book refer to a wide variety of recreational and educational activities that take place in an outdoor environment including boating in a city pond, camping in your backyard, hiking in a national forest, and backpacking on a wilderness trip. All outdoor activities involve using and not abusing our natural resources (plants, animals, land, air, or water) as part of that experience. Regardless of the activity, outdoor living skills are the skills needed for a meaningful outdoor experience with little or no impact on the environment.

What's So Great About the Great Outdoors?

To help others understand the importance of living in the outdoors and taking responsible action to minimize our impact on the environment, we need to understand why the outdoors is so significant. What's so great about the great outdoors?

Outdoor activities are among the most popular forms of recreation worldwide. We are fascinated by people who dare to scale a mountain, are enthralled with the competition of adventure racing, and revel in the thought of participating in "survival" activities. Although many of us will never summit Mt. Everest, raft the wilds of the Amazon, or live in the Outback, the outdoors is a place where you can have adventures, test your skills, and venture into unknown territory, even if only in your own backyard.

Today many people choose an outdoor experience to get away from it all, away from the smog, noise, and traffic of the city. In most cases, getting out into the great outdoors allows us to leave behind the TVs, VCRs, DVDs, computers, cell phones, telephones, e-mail, voice mail, snail mail, teleconferencing, video learning, web chatting, messaging, forwards, replies, video games, and other electronic "necessities" that have become so much a part of the stress and pressure of our daily lives. Like many others who enjoy outdoor living, you might say that the outdoors represents a certain amount of freedom; there are no walls or ceilings, so you don't feel hemmed in. Or perhaps you talk about the clean, fresh air or the beauty and serenity of nature. Whatever draws you to the outdoors, the same things probably appeal to other people. Without careful management of this fragile environment, its beauty and serenity can be transformed into crowded, blighted outdoor slums. Sharing your thoughts about outdoor ethics and the appeal of outdoor living with others, especially children and young people, will help them learn to appreciate it, too.

The Outdoor Environment

When we think of the term "environment" we often conjure up images of a beautiful forest with a lake or running stream, mountains or meadows, birds singing, and animals scurrying around. But the environment can mean different things to different people.

The environment is defined as "**a**: the complex of physical, chemical, and biotic factors (as climate, soil, and living things) that act upon an organism or an ecological community and ultimately determine its form and survival **b**: the aggregate of social and cultural conditions that influence the life of an individual or community" (Merriam-Webster, 2001). The environment is essentially all around us, where we live, play, and recreate.

Everyone has a different idea about what the outdoor environment means. The differences are wide and varied depending on where you live and your experience and comfort level. For example, people who live in a rural setting might consider the outdoors or the natural environment to be a running stream, rolling meadow, or even the pond on the farm. They may have grown up hunting, fishing, backpacking, hiking, and learning to live in an outdoor environment. Conversely, people who come from an urban or suburban setting would consider their local park, backyard, an empty lot, or even a drainage canal to be

Cheley Colorado Camps

Cheley Colorado Camps

Camp Slisson, Georgia

part of the natural environment. Some urban children have opportunities through school camping experiences to have an outdoor experience, but many without such exposure to the natural environment can be frightened by it because of what they view through movies and the media.

People Who Enjoy the Outdoors

Living in an outdoor environment dates back to the dawn of time. Ever since humankind has been on the earth, it has worked to survive and live in harmony with the natural environment. Gradually, humans learned to protect themselves from the elements: building shelters and making clothes. Eventually, they became indoor dwellers; however, people still went outdoors to hunt and gather food and, eventually, to spend time recreating outdoors. Today, nine of every ten Americans participate in some form of outdoor recreation every year.

Outdoor recreation can include hiking, biking, skiing, swimming, fishing, canoeing, kayaking, bird watching, and camping to name but a few activities. Camping in the simplest of terms really means housekeeping outdoors, and it can take several hours or several days of your time. However, no matter which activities we pursue outdoors, we should approach them with minimal impact to the environment.

Some people enjoy outdoor experiences alone, but many especially find it rewarding to share the experience with others. You may wonder, then, if people who enjoy outdoor activities have any common characteristics. The answer is yes. Both leaders and members of a group may already have or be able to develop the necessary traits. Characteristics most common among outdoor enthusiasts include

- wanting to be outdoors,

- enjoying being away from home overnight,

- being willing to be cooperative members of a group,

- having a spirit of adventure,

- getting along without total privacy,

- being willing to follow instructions,

- being able to take care of their belongings,

- enjoying the challenge of housekeeping outdoors, and

- enjoying participating in activity.

Of course, not everyone is immediately enthusiastic about being outdoors. Some people may take more time to adjust to unfamiliar settings if they have spent time in the outdoors before. For example, a participant from the inner city of Chicago who has never been in a rural environment might take some time to become accustomed to the night noises and lighting, which sound and look different than they do at home. Participants who live in more residential suburban areas, which are away from the city, might never have had the opportunity to venture into a natural area. They might be so afraid of such creatures as bats, raccoons, or even spiders that their fear will affect their experience. If they are uncomfortable in their new surroundings, they may not be paying attention to the content of the program.

A good leader will help participants gain a better understanding of the environment in which they are living. With time and patience, even the most reluctant person may learn to enjoy the outdoors. Much of this change may come about because of the understanding and consideration of the leader and others in the group. Participants may not have equal interest in, enthusiasm for, or knowledge of the outdoors, but you can help them develop their interests and skills beyond the ones they brought to the program. Through a program of progression, the additional experience, skills, and support will help them be more comfortable and enthusiastic about the outdoor experience.

Choosing a Place to Go

Where you go depends on your location, your available resources, and the experience level of your group. If you have a group that is not very skilled in living in an outdoor environment, you will want to choose a place that has more developed camping or picnic sites and bathrooms close by. If participants are more experienced with their skills, they will be more comfortable in the outdoors, and you may choose a place less accessible by vehicle with primitive sites or no developed sites at all. Whether you live in a rural environment or an urban environment, plenty of places for teaching outdoor living skills should be at yoru disposal. This can include national parks, national forests, state parks, summer camps, and year-round outdoor education or group facilities, and even city parks, picnic areas, and playgrounds. Outdoor living skills can be practiced almost anywhere, even in your own backyard.

Among the best places to go are the thousands of youth and adult camps in the United States and Canada and throughout the world. Camps can be found in the private or not-for-profit sector and can include organizations such as the Boy Scouts of America, Girl Scouts of the USA, YMCA, Camp Fire USA, Boys and Girls Clubs, 4-H, and numerous religious-affiliated organizations. Camp facilities can be found in every state and in all kinds of settings, including urban and rural, and day or overnight programs. Many camps also serve as environmental education centers during the school year and have facilities available for user groups that teach programs such as OLS.

If you are not familiar with the camps in this country, contact the American Camping Association for information. The ACA can tell you how to find camps that either specialize in outdoor living skills or have outdoor living skills as part of their program, or they can suggest facilities that you can use for your program.

On the national level, the U.S. Forest Service manages more than 100,000 miles of trails in 155 national forests and 20 grasslands located in 44 states, Puerto Rico, and the U.S. Virgin Islands. The Bureau of Land Management manages thousands of acres west of the Mississippi River, and many of those areas are available for camping. Also, the U.S. Army Corps of Engineers operates some camping sites and leases many others to counties.

The National Park System of the United States is composed of 384 areas covering more than 83 million acres in 49 states, the District of Columbia, American Samoa, Guam, Puerto Rico, Saipan, and the Virgin Islands. You can enjoy an excellent outdoor living experience at a national park. However, don't expect to be able to use all your outdoor living skills in every national park; many parks have historical or scientific importance, and as a result, visitors' activities may be restricted.

Consider visiting a federal wildlife refuge. Most wildlife refuges do not permit camping, but you can observe wildlife, take photographs, study nature, and go hiking or pursue other similar outdoor activities. So many places offer outdoor recreation that it's impossible to list them all. Finally, every state and nearly every county offers public parks. Most federal, state, and county lands permit people to cook outdoors, explore the grounds, and camp overnight at designated sites. In some areas, you are not permitted to gather wood so you must furnish your own, bring charcoal for designated fire pits, or use a camp stove. Traveling into the backcountry of some areas will allow you to practice more advanced skills. Contact your local land manager or Department of Natural Resources for more information on areas available and rules for use.

Appendix A lists other resources for choosing a place to go.

Camp Pemigewassett, New Hampshire

Cheley Colorado Camps

Cheley Colorado Camps

How Participants Travel

You need to consider two different kinds of transportation — that for getting to the area and that for getting around while at the site. Getting to an outdoor recreation area usually requires some type of motorized transportation — planes, buses, trains, or automobiles, depending on where you conduct your program. Some people, however, walk or travel there by mountain bike, boat, or horseback. At your designated site, participants can travel by various means, generally under their own power, which can include biking, hiking, horseback, canoeing, kayaking, or even sailing. Remember to take into account the age and physical condition of group members when structuring your outdoor activities so that they can enjoy the experience and not be overwhelmed by the amount of physical activity.

Consider the experience level of the participants not only with their outdoor living skills but also their experience on the mode of transportation you choose to use. If participants have minimal experience in a canoe, you may want to plan short paddles with limited portages. Depending on the length of the trip, you can increase the number of miles you paddle, hike, or bike after participants are comfortable. Whether you walk, paddle, or ride, use good judgment about how far you can expect to go in one day. As the leader, you must know how far your group can travel (include enough time and energy to get back to base camp if that is the plan).

The Next Step

You've planned how to get to your site and how to move from place to place on your trip. Now let's look at other possible activities. The list of favorite outdoor activities is long and varied. While many participants want to learn all they can about the area — its rocks, plants, animals, waterfalls, land formations, weather, and so forth — others want to explore the area using a map and compass, and others may simply want to rest and look at the scenery. Outdoor activities can be sedentary, such as writing poetry or telling stories, or active, such as picking berries for making pies or pancakes. Other activities may include rock climbing, canoeing, hiking, cross-country skiing, snow-shoeing, fishing, beachcombing, bird watching, taking photographs, sketching, singing, catching butterflies, and searching for Native American artifacts.

Be sure to include all members of your group in decision making not just in regard to the actual trip but also in regard to activities while on the trip. As a result, no one does only the thing he or she selects but is exposed to a wider variety of activities and experiences. This course of action enforces a sense of fairness and community. Remember that you are part of a bigger community; respect your neighbors both the two- and four-footed kind.

Being Comfortable

For many people, outdoor experiences are unfamiliar and foreign. These people aren't comfortable outdoors because they've never had any experience doing things in an environment where there are no telephones, stores, traffic noises, and other things to which they are accustomed. After all, indoor toilets, flowing tap water, refrigerators, microwave ovens, screens on the windows, and heating and air conditioning are customary. Cooking over an outdoor stove, using an outside bathroom, purifying water for drinking, sleeping in a tent, and worrying about skunks, snakes, and other things that go bump in the night are all new experiences for first-time participants. Some may have had a bad experience in the past whether they encountered mosquitoes or poison ivy, didn't know how to dress properly, or brought too much or too little equipment. Perhaps they found the outdoors to be too hot, too cold, too dirty, too buggy, too unfamiliar, or just too boring. A good leader will plan to make the experience as comfortable and rewarding as possible for all.

As human beings, we have specific needs that must be met if we are to live comfortably in any environment. To help do so, we need to look at two different comfort factors — physical and psychological. Outdoor living skills apply to both.

Physical Comfort

The first consideration for most participants is physical comfort or how a person feels when in an outdoor environment. Are they cold, hot, hungry, thirsty, or tired?

Things that make people physically comfortable are proper body temperature maintained by appropriate clothing and shelter, adequate safe drinking water, adequate rest and sleep, and sufficient amounts of high-energy food. It is the leader's responsibility to make sure that each participant is in physical condition for the planned activities and ready and well prepared for the trip or event.

Helpful Hint

Have additional clothing and supplies on hand for those just-in-case moments when a participant has forgotten to bring something or just doesn't have it.

Psychological Comfort

Psychological comfort refers to how people feel mentally and emotionally. Perhaps our greatest psychological need is the assurance that our biological needs have been met. If the group is physically comfortable and has the proper equipment to maintain this comfort, then mentally and emotionally, they'll be more inclined to feel good about their situation and responsive to the outdoors.

Our second greatest psychological need is knowing that we are safe both physically and emotionally. Participants need to know that where they are going is a safe place and the people they are going with (especially the leader) will afford a safe environment. Knowing that we're not going to be harassed or ridiculed by other members of the group or the public plays an integral part in our emotional security. Members need to feel assured that there is safety in being part of the group.

Third on the list of psychological needs is a sense of belonging, which contributes to a person's need for love or being a part of the group. Every member of the group needs to feel that he or she is wanted and can make a contribution, that the leader accepts him or her, and that the other group members feel that they can rely on him or her. Make sure that everyone feels that she or he belongs, is participating in the activities, and is a competent member of the group. Be aware of participants who are quiet, not interacting with others (particularly if they are new to an already established group), not wanting to participate, hanging back from the rest of the group, or letting others do everything. Facilitate learning experiences that help participants become involved and increase their understanding and skills, which in turn increase their self-esteem, self-confidence, and self-worth.

Keep in mind that you should never ridicule or undermine your group members' efforts. Never play practical jokes on the group or try to frighten them, and do not tolerate members frightening each other. Never do anything that would destroy the confidence that group members must have in you and the trust they have built with you.

Meeting all these different needs will help participants become more comfortable in the outdoor environment. Make sure that everyone in your group participates in the activities and feels secure both physically and psychologically so that each has a positive and comfortable experience, which can lead to lifelong outdoor pursuits.

Skills Participants Need

Participants will need to know a wide variety of skills to be physically and psychologically comfortable and safe in the outdoors. They include

- how to take care of themselves;

- what equipment they need, why they need it, and how to use it;

- how to keep from getting lost;

- how to find potable (safe) water;

- how to pack, prepare, and store food;

- how to use a stove safely;

- how to read and follow a map;

- how to handle an emergency, which includes a basic understanding of the importance of first aid and certification from a nationally recognized body that teaches first aid; and

- how to function competently and responsibly in a natural environment.

The rest of this book discusses skills needed to live comfortably in the outdoors and information on how to teach others those skills. You should read the book from front to back without jumping around between chapters. A list of references at the end of the book may help you increase your knowledge of those skills.

Leadership Strategies

Cheley Colorado Camps

Leadership and teaching go hand in hand. To be an effective teacher, you need to develop strong leadership skills and understand group dynamics. This chapter not only describes what it means to be a leader and identifies different leadership styles but also talks about group leadership and ties it in with teaching methods and learning styles. All these topics will factor into a positive outdoor experience for both you and the participants learning outdoor living skills.

Leadership

Leadership skills can be divided into three categories — technical skills, human relations skills, and conceptual skills. Effective leaders work to improve and combine these skills in ways that will help their group accomplish its goals.

- Technical skills are specific to accomplishing tasks. Individuals with technical skills know how to perform the tasks required to get the job done. However, having the skill does not mean that one can motivate and teach others. For example, a good swimmer may not be able to teach others to swim.

- Human relations skills involve interaction with others and include good communications skills, an understanding of group dynamics, and the ability to facilitate cooperation and trust, inspire and motivate people, and help them to feel valued and respected.

- Conceptual skills encompass the ability to communicate and share the vision. They include helping the group members know what the results of their work will be, why it is important, and how you plan to get there. Conceptual skills involve the ability to analyze, anticipate, and use critical thinking and problem-solving skills.

Three Prominent Styles of Leadership

As leaders acquire skills, they must determine the most effective way to combine these skills and select a style of leadership most appropriate for the group and the situation. Three basic styles of leadership are described in Table 2-1.

Table 2-1 Leadership Styles and Characteristics

Style	Leader Characteristics	Effective	Ineffective
Benevolent Autocratic	Skilled, experienced, relies on authority, makes decisions, tells others what to do, maintains control, high concern for task and lower concern for people	When time is limited, group lacks skill and knowledge, there is an emergency situation, group is motivated, members of group do not know each other	When team-building is the goal, members of the group have skills and knowledge, group wants some say or spontaneity
Democratic (Participative)	Good knowledge of group and task, involves group in decisions, fair, good listener, shares responsibility and authority, empowers others, focuses on how the team is accomplishing the task	When time is available, the group is motivated and functioning as a team; group has some confidence, skills, and knowledge	When the group is unmotivated, high degree of conflict is present, time is limited, group members do not know each other
Free-Rein (Laissez-Faire)	Gives up control, only offers opinion when asked, trusts the group's ability, has no sense of being in charge, relaxed, inconclusive, relinquishes authority, and nonjudgmental	When there is a high degree of skill and motivation, routine is familiar to group, sense of team exists, no time constraints, everyone has an equal say, creative thinking by the group is desired, autonomous groups	When the group expects to be told what to do, group lacks needed skills and knowledge, group fails to cooperate, group is coming together for the first time unless strong leadership emerges

The first type of leadership style is benevolent autocratic. These people concentrate on the task at hand with little recognition of how the group is working together or the relationships within the group. An example might be a leader who says, "I understand you're tired, but we need to get this done."

The next leadership style is democratic. Democratic leaders rate high on the task scale and high on the relationship scale. They focus on group goals and objectives but encourage individuals to meet their personal goals and objectives. There is a concern for building relationships and working together on the process of succeeding in the task. A democratic leader may say, "I understand that you are tired so let's sit down and talk about what is needed to complete the task and meet our goals and objectives."

The last leadership style is free-rein. This type of leader is the opposite of the democratic leader. Free-rein leaders are not concerned with relationships or the task. They give out the task and let the group take care of itself. They are rarely seen monitoring the group or checking on goals and objectives. This allows the team with experience and motivation to make its own decisions and to deal with the consequences of those decisions. A laissez-faire leader would say, "We need to get to Sunset Point by 5 P.M.; you decide how to get there."

Other Leadership Styles or Combinations

Most people who study leadership believe that choosing an appropriate leadership style depends on a number of factors including the leader's experience and comfort level, the stage of group development, the age and/or experience of the group, and the situation.

Inexperienced leaders or leaders who have a desire to be part of the in-group are easily persuaded to conform to the group's desire in order to be liked. They are more concerned with wanting everyone to be happy and often fall into the trap of losing focus or interest in the task. Sometimes the situation should dictate the appropriate style; however, leadership style is important at other times.

When safety is an issue, an autocratic leadership style is generally most appropriate. The leader gives directions and does not immediately explain the reasons. If the purpose is to enhance and empower group process and development, a free-rein or consensus style of leadership might be most appropriate. Using this style, the leader purposely steps back so that the group can struggle with decision making and norm setting. This approach to leadership is quite common in group initiatives and ropes or challenge courses. The group is given a task, and the leader serves only as a safety net or resource; the group must do all the work and establish its own group norms and behaviors.

The real challenge is to understand and become a situational leader — someone who uses the appropriate leadership style to fit the group and the situation. Although there certainly are individual comfort levels in using particular leadership styles over others, understanding and being able to use all types is necessary. Bear in mind that not all styles are equally effective with all people. As with leaders, participants are more comfortable with and have a better response to certain types of leadership.

Leading Strategy

Establishing trust is one of the most important components of successful teaching and leadership. Trust can't be bought or transferred; rather, it must be earned. Trust is essential in any leadership situation, and participants will find it easier to communicate and work together as a group after trust is established. Trust allows for a better learning process because participants have developed a comfort factor with one another.

To work toward trust:

- Begin with get-acquainted activities. They help participants learn one another's names and feel more comfortable in their surroundings.

- Get on their level. Participants will feel more at ease if you speak and interact with them on their level. If you have small participants, kneel down in front of them so that they can see you face to face and do not have to look up at you.

- Use eye contact.

- Keep your voice well modulated. Be enthusiastic, even when you don't feel your best, and use humor when appropriate.

- Get and hold their attention. Don't start talking until you have the attention of the participant or group.

- Listen to comments and try to understand them. Remember that what people say isn't always what they mean.

- Participate in learning with the group when appropriate but don't overshadow them with your expertise or dominate the discussion or activity. Sometimes it is good to let the group learn from one another, but be prepared to step in if there is inaccurate information being presented.

- Admit when you are wrong. Participants need to understand that it is okay to make mistakes and that acknowledging one's errors is admirable.

- Try to make everything, even mistakes, a learning experience. Conversely, if trust is stripped from a participant or group (not following through with what you said you would do, mocking or making fun of participants, not admitting mistakes when participants know otherwise), the group's respect for and trust in the leader will be severely damaged. Participants who have experienced distrust (whether in your group or at another time) are less likely to actively participate, will have a harder time with the activity and trusting those around them, and will not have a meaningful experience.

The role you take as the leader is critical to the group's success. Learning depends on the attitude of the group, as well as on your attitude and actions, in terms of guidance, organization, coordination, delegation of authority, respect, and dependability. Group members have greater trust in leaders whom they perceive to be fair, considerate, and consistent. If you have all these qualities, the group's morale and efficiency will be high, and group members will be inclined to imitate your favorable personality characteristics, such as camaraderie and friendliness.

Your group can see you as both a leader and a friend. Too often, leaders aspire to be best friends with the group members and so lose sight of their roles as leaders; when they do, they face making decisions that compromise their responsibility, authority, and integrity. An effective leader can juggle the delicate balance of traits and skills. A list of common leadership characteristics follows.

Decision-making ability. A good leader has the ability to make decisions efficiently and effectively. A leader needs to be able to make a decision based on what is in the best interest of the group, the task at hand, and at times safety elements.

Confidence. A good leader is confident of her or his decisions but is open to additional information that could change the decision. A good leader needs to be confident in all aspects of leadership including group management, skills, ability, and decision making.

Enthusiasm. Enthusiasm is contagious. When you're excited and interested, the group becomes excited and interested.

Positive attitude. A leader's attitude is also contagious. If you exhibit a poor attitude toward an activity or task, the group will reflect that attitude. Conversely, having a positive attitude increases the group's morale, reflects in their attitude, and sparks enthusiasm for other activities.

Respect for other people. A good leader respects all members of the group, whatever their abilities, attitudes, and opinions and differences. Each member of the group is an individual first and as such deserves all the respect you can give. Respect reciprocates respect.

Problem-solving ability. A good leader sees problems as opportunities for growth rather than as obstacles. Too often, groups and leaders spend more time thinking about why they can't do something than what they can do. If you see a glass as being half full rather than half empty, you're likely to view a problem as being a challenge rather than an obstacle.

Punctuality. A good leader respects time and uses it to his or her advantage. Notify the group when an activity will start, start on time, tell the group how long the activity will last, and end on time. If you find that the activity is taking longer than you expected, don't extend the time without first getting the group's agreement and then taking a break before continuing on.

Planning skills. A good leader always works from a plan, which is a road map to success. Remain focused but flexible and allow for unexpected diversions and complications because inevitably they will arise.

Recognition of strengths and weaknesses. Everyone has strengths and weaknesses. A good leader recognizes his or her own strengths and weaknesses as well as those of group members. Reward strengths and things a participant does well, through compliments or other means such as completion patches or certificates. Conversely a good leader also recognizes weaknesses in participants and helps them to improve their skills or abilities. Leaders can recognize their own weaknesses and determine the best means of improving them through skill building and practice or by enlisting assistance from another individual.

Listening skills. Listening skills are the key to clear communication. A lack of communication between you and your group may result in poor learning, misunderstandings, and a reduced enjoyment of the outdoors. In some instances, it could also pose a safety hazard (i.e., using tools incorrectly). Communication is a two-way process. While one person is sending a message, the other is receiving. You can communicate in several different ways including words, voice tone or inflection, body language, facial expressions, attentiveness, and eye contact. The following activities present some common obstacles to listening:

ACA File Photo

- talking (you can't talk and listen at the same time);

- thinking about what you want to say while the other person is speaking;

- mentally arguing with the person who is talking;

- mentally criticizing the speaker's grammar, appearance, and the like;

- failing to receive the entire message (gestures, expressions, intonation, and other nonverbal signals);

- putting your mind in neutral when someone is talking;

- being preoccupied with another task;

- trying to listen in a poor environment (visual distractions or noise, uncomfortable room temperature or seating, etc.);

- being mentally or physically fatigued.

Use the following suggestions to help develop listening skills and clear communication:

- Maintain eye contact with the individual.

- Nod that you understand and hear what the speaker is saying.

- Confirm what you heard by saying something like, "So what I hear you telling me is that you're not happy with . . . Is that right?"

- If not in the same room or if using the phone, verbally give a signal that you are in tune with what they are saying (uh-huh, yes, etc).

- Put away or turn off all things that could cause distraction (pen and paper, telephones, television, computers, etc.).

- Don't interrupt. Wait for the person to finish his or her statement or thought before giving your own thoughts or feedback.

Knowing Your Audience

One of the first tasks as a leader is to understand who your group members are and where they are from. Where do they live? What is their economic status? What is their perception of the natural environment? What experience or skill level do they have? How do they learn? Participants in the OLS program will come from many different communities and are diverse in many other ways. Some may be rural, urban, or suburban. Some may be from more affluent communities, while other participants might come from a lower economic background. Some might be older and have more experience and ability. The mix of people participating in outdoor activities is wide and varied. People from all ages and different walks of life take part in outdoor pursuits. Understanding the diversity of the group you will be working with (ability, age, ethnicity, experience, geographic location) is a key to providing successful education in outdoor living skills.

Ability. Ability is what participants are capable of doing. For example, a ten-year-old participant is better able to learn how to light a camp stove properly than someone who is six or seven years old. Whether they are new to this type of program, have taken part in a formal program, or have learned at home from family and friends, assessing individuals on the skills they know (versus the skills they think they know) is important. In a group of ten participants, no two participants will have exactly the same skills.

Age. Participants in outdoor living skills programs can range in age from the very young to the very old. The OLS program is designed for children as young as five to learn new skills, and they do so successfully. In the same regard, the program can be used for participants who might be older and want to learn new skills. Taking age into account can be a critical factor when planning an OLS program — not only for what you teach but also for how you teach it.

Diversity. The United States is a melting pot of different races and cultures. Outdoor recreation is growing nationally and internationally. Consequently, more participants bring with them a variety of different experiences, which may have an impact on their participation in the program. As an example, some races and cultures may not have a history of valuing the outdoor experience, while others are very comfortable with living in an outdoor environment. However comfortable, they may not have the information or concern about how to do so with the least amount of impact on the environment. For example, they might be highly skilled at fishing and keep what they catch for eating, not realizing that there are regulations in place regarding the size and number of fish they are allowed to keep so that a good stock in the lake can be maintained. It is important to open the experience of learning outdoor skills to all people and to understand how different values and cultures may affect or contribute to the program.

Energy and Strength. Energy and strength can vary from participant to participant or even from participant to leader. Some participants might have more endurance and stamina than others. A seventeen year old will probably be able to go farther on a hike than someone who is very young or a senior citizen. However, older adults may have more stamina and endurance if the seventeen year old has never been on a hike before or is in poor physical condition. Younger children tend to have short bursts of energy and speed but might tire in a short amount of time. People who are in good shape, exercise routinely, and eat properly and those who feel no apprehension tend to move faster than those who exercise less, are out of shape, are frightened by their surroundings, or are just plain uncomfortable. When you plan an activity, take into account the fact that participants' energy and strength can vary and may require an adjustment to your program.

Experience Level. Chalk up experience level to the amount of times they have used their skills or how well they know their skills. For example, participants who were taught to pitch a tent with a group at a summer camp but never did it on their own may have a lower experience level than others who learned the skill from their families and participated in camping trips every weekend of the summer. Experience level can play a critical role in the direction of your program. For example, if one participant has more experience than the rest of the group, you as a leader can use that person to help demonstrate skills and assist in teaching the class. If you have several participants who are quite skilled and pick up information easily, you might be able to teach skills more quickly than expected.

People with Disabilities. As with energy and strength, it is important to focus on participants' abilities, not their disabilities. A disability can be thought of as a restriction that challenges the person to function differently than someone without a disability. People with visual impairments, hearing impairments, mental or physical challenges, or even learning disabilities may have special needs that you must address to help them enjoy the program. You may need to adjust the way you teach to help them be more successful and learn. For example, someone who is visually impaired might be teamed with a sighted person to cook a meal, and if someone is confined to a wheelchair, you must select an accessible site.

Size. Participants can vary greatly in size. For example, sixth graders vary in height by as much as 18 inches and can vary in weight by as much as a hundred pounds. Adults, too, exhibit many differences in size and shape. These differences can affect how you put together your program. Some people may be unable to reach the stepping stones that others use to cross a creek or unable to wear other people's backpacks without the packs bumping the backs of their thighs. Plan for the smallest and weakest participants as well as for those who are large and strong.

Where They Live

Children today may have a view of the outdoor environment more from what they see on television and in the movies than from actual experiences. Such programs may help instill an environmental awareness or real fear of the environment. Knowing where your participants live will help you plan and teach the OLS program. Participants can come from rural, suburban, and urban communities.

Rural participants (small towns, farms, or forest areas) are familiar with what we typically define as an outdoor community (the lake, woods, animals in a remote environment). Many have had the opportunity to participate in activities — whether through school, community, or family — that exposes them to an outdoor or natural environment simply out of need or because of where they live. If they live on a family farm, they probably help out with such chores as feeding the animals or working in the garden. They might also be familiar with such outdoor sounds as owls hooting and crickets chirping and are used to seeing wild animals near their homes.

Suburban participants are a hybrid between rural and urban dwellers. Suburban participants tend to live in more city-like environments and are located on the outskirts of the city limits or just outside a city community. They may or may not have been exposed to a more natural environment such as a forest or meadow in their immediate living areas, but they have probably been exposed to parks, which could have ponds, lakes, or hiking trails.

Urban participants live in the city itself. Participants who come from these environments may have very little exposure to a rural environment. Like their neighbors in the suburbs, they might have exposure to park areas depending on what part of the city they come from, or they may never have even been out of their neighborhood. They may or may not have participated in school outdoor education or field trips.

All these factors will influence how you teach outdoor living skills. Knowing where your participants live, their experience level, and even their age can influence where you choose to go, what skills you plan to teach, and how you plan to teach them.

How They Learn

Years ago children were sent to a one-room schoolhouse and expected to learn the same material by the same method. Today, research has proven that individuals learn in a variety of ways using various techniques that help enhance retention and understanding. Good leaders understand not only who their audience is but also that each person may learn differently than the next, and will adjust their teaching to meet all needs.

How do we learn? Does everyone respond to the same technique? Do all of us comprehend the same lesson in the same way? What about the information given? Do we all understand everything that we are told when we are learning a new activity? Do I do better working with a group or working more independently?

It has long been known that children as well as adults learn in a variety of ways. What might prove an easy task for some when they are given verbal instructions may seem completely impossible for someone else.

Three Styles of Learning

There are essentially three styles of learning — visual, auditory, and tactile. They can be used independently or in a combination to provide an optimum learning experience.

- Visual learners learn best by seeing how things are done either by example or with charts, graphs, and videos.

- Auditory learners learn best when the instructions or directions are explained to them. They hear what they need to do or how to do it.

- Tactile learners can also be called "hands-on learners." The best way to process information is to actually do the skill or activity.

Every person uses each of these styles in some form or another when learning. However, one style is usually predominant. Typically most OLS skills are hands-on, since participants need to practice them to become skilled. Whatever the process of learning best benefits your group, one thing is certain: outdoor living skills allow you the opportunity to use a variety of these techniques while teaching.

Because participants learn at varying speeds, you should use a variety of different techniques to accommodate all learning styles. Other factors can come into play such as age (e.g., younger participants have a shorter attention span than older participants). Another consideration might be learning differences. Even though everyone has a different learning style, some might be diagnosed with a learning disability (or can be considered learning different), which will affect their participation and the outcome of the program.

People learn best when they're interested in the information, when they understand the value of the information, and when they actually participate in activities and become involved in teaching other people. Be aware that these factors exist, and be prepared to teach using a variety of different techniques.

Keep in mind that everyone makes mistakes. Just remember that you were a beginner once. Don't be afraid to ask questions of a more experienced person or to admit that you don't know the answer when someone asks you a question. If you don't know the answer, make it a habit to find the answer for your participants at a later time.

General Tips for Leading a Group

Leadership is a learned behavior that is acquired through formal and informal experiences. Just as you become an experienced teacher by teaching, you become an experienced leader by leading. The OLS program provides a unique opportunity for developing both teaching and leading skills.

Nearly all outdoor living skills instruction occurs in a group setting. The following sections provide tips on teaching in the group setting.

Preparing

Preparation is a key to having a successful program. Knowing what you are going to do and when you will be doing it is important.

- Create a short outline for yourself, listing the topics you want to cover in the order you want to cover them.

- Practice your teaching skills and be prepared to make some changes to accommodate your group.

- Check out the area before starting. Familiarize yourself with the site, and preview the materials and equipment available.

- Have all equipment and teaching materials ready and in working condition.

- Have a backup plan! Decide what you will do in case of rain, snow, wind, blinding sunshine, too many or too few participants, equipment failure, and so on.

- Look at your organization's risk management plan. In the event of an emergency or crisis that might develop, you should know the procedures to follow to provide a safe environment and to get your group to safety if need be.

Involving Participants

Participant involvement is a key to success. Participants who are involved in the process are willing to share their experiences in discussions and are more likely to learn.

- Seat participants so that they can see one another. Try seating people in a circle, square, or horseshoe; such an arrangement makes eye contact easier and gives everyone a sense of belonging to the group.

- Never stand in the middle of the circle, square, or horseshoe yourself. Join the group.

- When you use a table for a demonstration, have the group gather around you.

- Don't put a barrier between yourself and the group by standing behind the table.

- If outside, place the sun in your face, not in the faces of the participants, so that they can fully see you or what you are doing.

- Let participants answer other participant's questions. It's your responsibility, however, to add or to ask for information if a participant's response is not complete or accurate.

- When you ask questions, avoid asking those that have "yes" or "no" answers; ask for explanations, suggestions, and alternatives. Don't get impatient; wait for someone to answer. It may take some time at first.

- Acknowledge each group member's response, and invite discussion of those responses, whenever possible. Instead of saying that a response is right or wrong, good or bad, ask for other ideas.

- Get the group to share several answers, and discuss why some are more appropriate than others.

Group Planning and Decision Making

ACA File Photo

As mentioned previously, having a plan is a roadmap to success for any leader or group. Group participation in the decision-making process will not only make them feel that they have input into decisions but also make them feel important and that their opinion is important. Seven ways to make a group decision include

- group consensus,

- majority vote,

- small group representing a larger group,

- averaging opinions of the group,

- relying on an expert in the group,

- relying on an appointment authority in the group to decide after other members have made their recommendations, and

- relying on some authority outside the group who has no personal involvement in it.

Group participants have many different talents and strengths, which can be utilized for the benefit of everyone.

Clearly identify the purpose. The discussion topic, problem, or activity may be determined either by you or by the group.

Identify the conditions necessary to accomplish the goals.
What needs to happen or be in place? Consider conditions such
as time, space, materials, cost, people, and skills.

Revise the goals. After you identify the conditions necessary to
accomplish the group's goals, you may find that those goals
need to be adjusted.

Develop a written plan. Diagram the conditions you identified,
including specific elements involved in completing the task. For
example, if the goal is to prepare meals for an overnight trip,
your diagram might look like the following:

- What. Plan menus for one dinner, one breakfast, and one
  lunch. Purchase all food supplies for menus and pack them
  for trip.

- How. Divide group into three smaller groups, assigning each
  group one meal. After meals are planned, combine all grocery
  lists so that groceries can be purchased by a select group of
  people. After shopping has been completed, divide and pack
  food supplies in order of the meals to be eaten.

- Who. The entire group will help plan menus in three smaller
  groups and will select a small group to go with leader to
  grocery store.

- How much. The number of people in the group will determine
  the amount of food. The type of food may be determined by
  dollar amount allotted to spend. Plan for at least 1 ½ servings
  per person for a typical adult.

- When. The menu plan must be complete one week in
  advance of trip. Grocery shopping must be completed at
  least one day in advance of trip. Packing will take place the
  morning of departure. Put the plan into action. Follow the
  objectives that you have created.

Evaluate. Evaluation is an on-going process. As progress or lack
of progress is made, information is collected, and decisions are
constantly revised. For example, as the group is grocery shopping, they discover that the price of English muffins has gone
up and that they will not be able to afford them based on their
budget. They decide to replace the muffins with bagels. Objectives should be evaluated and re-evaluated. Will we meet the
time frames? Will we meet the budget? Why? Why not? How
can we make it work? Use checklists, reports, observations,
comparisons, or other formal and informal methods to evaluate
the success of the plan.

Generating and Sharing Ideas

Trust is a key factor if all members of the group are to share ideas. In the early stages, members will be somewhat tentative, shy, and perhaps even fearful of participating in the group, and spontaneous discussion won't occur naturally. As the group works together and its members become more comfortable with one another, the trust factor increases as does participation in group discussion and group tasks.

You can use a variety of methods when leading groups. Some methods are more suitable to particular situations than others. For example, holding a group discussion about how to tie knots is probably not as effective as actually tying knots together. Knowing when and why they need to tie the knot will make the learning session even more effective. Group discussion may, however, be appropriate when trying to decide whether to build a fire. Many of these methods allow participants to work either on their own or in small or large groups. Using a combination of these techniques will not only enhance the material being taught but also meet the different learning needs your participants might have.

Helpful Hint

A golden rule of thumb when teaching any material is to KIS it! Keep It Simple. Breaking down the material into simple steps is one of the best ways to enhance learning and retention.

Brainstorming

Brainstorming is a method of generating as many suggestions as possible in a short period of time. Proceed by following these steps:

- Identify the problem or issue.
- Set a reasonable time limit for offering suggestions.
- Tell group members that there are no "wrong" ideas and that there will be no discussion of ideas at this stage.
- Appoint someone to write down the ideas on a blackboard or other object that everyone can see.
- Share ideas.
- Stop when the time limit is reached or ideas are exhausted.
- Review the ideas.
- Eliminate obviously inappropriate ideas.
- Discuss and prioritize the remaining ideas.

Group Discussion

Group discussion can be a great tool in the learning process and can usually be used in any setting. When the group has been working individually or in small groups, it is particularly effective to bring everyone back together and summarize the end of a discussion. Productive group discussions depend on participation by all members of the group. Participation in a discussion will depend on each member's willingness to participate, understanding of the topic or material, motivation to contribute, and acceptance of responsibility for her or his actions.

Group discussion can take the form of either large group discussion or small group discussion (buzz groups). Both can be very effective. Large group discussion allows for the entire group to interact with one another, but some participants may feel intimidated by a large group and not give as much input as they might in a small group. Small group discussion allows people to interact in smaller numbers and gives a greater opportunity for everyone to have a chance to participate in the discussion. Sometimes in larger groups, due to the number of people and time constraints, not everyone who would like to speak will get the opportunity to do so.

Large Group Discussion

The following suggestions will help implement successful large group discussions and participation:

- Group members must agree on, or at least understand, the task, question, activity, or reason for being assembled.

- Group members must be able to communicate and be respectful of the opinions of other group members, even if they don't agree.

- Group members must have some interest in the task.

- Group members should have sufficient time to complete the task or discussion.

- Group members should not feel that they're being forced to participate.

As a leader you need to keep the group focused; lack of focus results in wasted time, unproductive discussion, and failure to achieve the purpose of the discussion. Use your discretion.

Facilitate discussion by encouraging group members to participate and by giving them opportunities to do so. Asking questions is one of the best techniques for encouraging interaction.

Use the following suggestions to increase participation:

- State the purpose of the discussion.
- State any rules of conduct.
- Give a specific task or specific information.
- Encourage and praise participation.
- Mediate differences of opinion.
- Refocus the group's attention, when necessary.
- Clarify definitions.
- Provide relevant facts.
- Offer new ideas when group members have exhausted theirs.
- Check participants' willingness to accept new ideas.
- Summarize the discussion.

Buzz Groups

Using buzz groups involves breaking large groups into smaller ones for problem-solving purposes. To use the buzz group method, follow these steps:

- Define the problem or issue.
- Break the large group into smaller groups.
- Assign each group a specific task or part of a task.
- Set a time limit for completion of the task.
- Share ideas in small groups.
- Stop when the time limit is reached or ideas are exhausted.
- Return to the large group.
- Ask the small groups to report to the large group.
- Share any ideas or suggestions.
- Review.

Other Tips

Role Play

Role-playing is useful for visualizing an issue to understand it better. To use the role-playing method, follow these steps:

- Define the problem or issue.
- Explain what you want the group to achieve (e.g., to find more options or to clarify the problem).

- Establish the situation and the role players.

- Assign roles to group members.

- Set a time limit.

- Allow characters to play out the situation.

- Discuss and review the role-playing.

Observation

Helping people sharpen their observation skills creates excitement and makes learning fun. You can make observation be effective and fun in dozens of ways, including the following activities:

- taking a quiet night walk without flashlights so that participants can hear the sounds of night and discover how their eyes cope with darkness (make sure that you know the trail);

- looking at an insect under a microscope;

- lying on your belly on the ground, looking for tiny creatures;

- watching the morning sky for clouds;

- sitting quietly in the woods from dusk until dark, while day animals scurry to their homes and night animals begin to venture out;

- carefully breaking apart owl pellets to see what the owl has been eating;

- smelling the differences between pinecones and maple leaves;

- feeling the difference between granite and limestone;

- listening for woodpeckers; and

- playing observation games such as "I Spy," "Riddly, Riddly, Ree, I See Something You Don't See," and "Trust Walk." (Playing these games helps to increase group members' interest, curiosity, and enthusiasm and leads to other activities or discussion.)

Upon completion of a game or activity, ask the group members what they did that increased their observation skills (group discussion). Help members discuss both what they observed and how they observed it.

The following tips can improve group members' powers of observation:

- Define what group members will observe. Be as specific or vague as you like.

- Make sure that participants know the rules. Are they to be quiet? Do you want feedback during the observation, or only after the group has finished the observation?

- Build on and encourage comments at discussion time, be that during or after the observation.

- Encourage participants to use all their senses. Set up observations that require techniques other than viewing.

- Demonstrate observation techniques by pointing out various things in nature. Do this even while you are involved in other activities.

- Explain that observation is not identification — that you don't expect group members to know all the names of things.

- Ask participants to observe from different points of view, such as through a magnifying glass or binoculars, and from an ant's viewpoint or bird's viewpoint.

- Make up stories that make observation fun. For example, tell the group that 3-inch-tall aliens have landed at camp, using dragonflies as their airplanes.

Demonstration and Practice

Demonstration and practice help participants learn and retain information. Before demonstrating a skill to participants, practice with another leader. When you know a skill well, it is often difficult to remember to demonstrate it step by step. Doing a demonstration ahead of time will help you to break down the skills into simple steps for the participants to understand and practice.

Tips for a successful demonstration:

- Understand the skill fully.

- Break the skill into easy steps.

- Consider both right-handed and left-handed participants.

- Demonstrate slowly, matching your actions to your words. For example, if you're saying, "right hand does this," don't stand facing the group; the technique will look exactly opposite to them. In this case, it may be better to have learners look over your shoulder as you demonstrate.

- Enlarge or personalize the demonstration so that everyone can see what you're doing.

- Allow time for participants to practice each step, praising and reinforcing success.

- Repeat and review, checking the group's understanding of each step.

- Help everyone participate by making the demonstration and the practice session fun and nonthreatening.

- Ask participants to demonstrate the skill.

Helpful Hint

A simple method for demonstration and practice is the SIP method. Show, Instruct, Practice.

Show. At the beginning of teaching a skill, show the participants how the skill works.

Instruct. After you have shown the skill, do it again, but this time give them the instructions on how to do it while you are demonstrating the skill.

Practice. After you have shown the skill and given instruction, they need to practice the skill. Have each participant perform the skill and, as the instructor, you can walk around to everyone to observe and make corrections as needed. Always emphasize a positive comment before giving correction.

Managing Behavior

Inevitably when teaching outdoor living skills, you will need to deal with either individual or group behavior. This time can arise with either children or adults, but it is generally more prevalent with children. How you handle certain situations can have an impact on the outcome of the activity. Be quick to catch participants doing something properly, but should you need to deal with individual or group behavior use the following suggestions.

Dealing with the Inappropriate Behavior of Groups

Most incidents and accidents come when there is free time or participants are "horsing around." A well-planned activity, timed so that group members are not idle or bored while waiting on others, is key to preventing inappropriate behavior.

Before discipline becomes an issue, you should understand and accept the following basic facts about youth, teens, and young adults:

- They have the occasional need to test the limits.

- They cannot always manage self-control.

- They have a strong tendency to imitate the values of their peer group.

- They have the right to make mistakes.

- They have a right to be respected as an individual, regardless of unattractive attributes.

Helping participants understand your expectations can help prevent discipline problems. You need to earn their respect by giving respect and by maintaining control, listening and reading signals, and trying to be one step ahead of them.

Dealing with the Inappropriate Behavior of Individuals

If initial attempts to control or change an unacceptable behavior have failed, these processes may help:

- Maintain the initiative and try to persuade the individual that it is better to conform.

- Avoid specific threats by using a broad warning of a possible course of action. Rather than saying, "if you do that again, you will be sent home," try "there are consequences for breaking rules or for not cooperating." A specific threat commits you to carry it out or back down and may even dare the participant to test you, whereas a general warning reinforces the idea that compliance will be better than defiance.

- Review any punishment before setting it. Does it fit the offense? For example, if a participant has peppered another's dessert, is it fair that the culprit goes without his dessert? Is punishment necessary to deter a repetition of the behavior? Any persistently antisocial behavior should not be allowed to pass without some appropriate action. Some individuals respond better to negative consequences, whereas others respond better to rewards or positive reinforcement.

- Look for causes. Avoiding difficult situations is much better than dealing with them once they arise. Youth, teens, and young adults with too much energy can get into trouble; overtired ones are prone to react badly to provocation. If a participant is more prone to negative behavior, try to start each day in a manner that will encourage proper behavior. Try to identify individuals who might cause problems and have strategies in mind to deal with them; having a plan will keep the problems from seeming overwhelming. (The ACA Bookstore has detailed resources available from www.ACAcamps.com for handling specific behavioral issues in outdoor settings. For example, *Camp Is for the Camper* is a booklet on positive development and managing group and individual behavior.)

Good behavior management helps youth and teens know their limits, helps provide a safe experience, helps accomplish the goals of the activity, and meets the expectations of parents, staff members, volunteers, and organizations.

On Your Way

ACA File Photo

Before you can head out on your way, you need to consider many different things and make solid plans. This chapter is about understanding the outdoors, what it means to practice minimum impact skills, and what preparations must be made before going outdoors — what to take, how to select it, some things to do when you get there, and what to do so that you'll get home safely.

Minimum Impact Camping

To understand minimum impact camping, it is important to learn about the environment or create an environmental awareness. Environmental awareness is an understanding of our natural environment, our impact on the environment, and what things are and how they interact within the ecosystem. Environmental awareness then leads to sound environmental ethics or a guiding philosophy or what you believe about the environment. Why is this important in learning outdoor living skills? Outdoor living skills teach participants to live comfortably outdoors with minimal impact on the surrounding environment.

Today, hundreds of thousands of people enjoy camping and other outdoor pursuits. Many outdoor enthusiasts go to areas that have been popular for years and, as a result, have strained the ecosystem and polluted the environment. Simply defined, pollution is making something unclean with man-made materials. For example, if you left wrappings and garbage in the woods without throwing away in a proper receptacle, you would be polluting. Pollution can also include throwing waste products such as used oil or other chemical agents into a body of water such as a lake or stream. Minimum impact camping teaches participants to respect the environment, to leave the site with minimal or no impact, and to care for the environment appropriately while onsite.

Proper treatment of the environment includes considerations as simple as how you walk on a trail and when, where, and how you build a fire. If we all walked beside a muddy trail just to keep our hiking shoes clean from snow or mud, the trails would become unnaturally wide or an additional trail would be added. When we walk off trail, we trample down the grass and vegetation that is already there. This is a natural protection for the soil. If a footpath is established beside the trail and gets worn down, erosion of the soil can also take place through wind and water action. Practicing minimum impact camping skills will, for example, prevent the development of impact areas, such as unintentional development of trails and later erosion of the soil.

Minimum impact camping can be defined as using outdoor living skills that affect the soil, water, plants, and animals in an area as little as possible. This practice is also called "no-trace camping" or "low-impact camping." Minimum impact camping is based on the simple idea of going outdoors to become part of the natural world, rather than to use it for your benefit alone. A scientific concept called "carrying capacity" explains our relationship with the environment. Land, water, animals, and plants can stand only so much human impact before their quality becomes irreversibly diminished, or the ecosystem has reached its carrying capacity. It is our responsibility as stewards of the natural world to answer the questions: "How much and what kinds of activity can this place stand?" and "Will the proposed activity affect the environment in any way?" Talk with participants about carrying capacity and what determines when that capacity has been met. Include questions such as

- When is an area too crowded for privacy?

- How many people are capable of living on a particular site before there is impact on the surrounding environment?

- When do our actions affect the rest of the natural world?

- When is it too noisy for others who are camping in the same area?

- When is our experience diminished by the actions or presence of others?

Give participants an opportunity to talk about examples. By discussing minimum impact camping as a group, you begin the process of developing an environmental awareness and ethic. In turn, participants will make responsible decisions that will allow them to enjoy their outdoor environment comfortably and with minimal impact on the environment.

Choices, Decisions, and Values

We all make decisions on a daily basis, and each one of us has a responsibility to take care of the world in which we live. An important concept is to get participants to understand that everything they do (positive or negative) in an outdoor environment matters. The choices and decisions we make are based on the values and beliefs we have.

There are no hard and fast rules for minimum impact camping; the best way to camp differs from region to region. Camping practices that are best for the land in the Rocky Mountains may not be suitable for the land in the Sonoran Desert. Appropriate practices for the White Mountains of New Hampshire differ from those for the dunes of Michigan, the Smoky Mountains of Tennessee and North Carolina, the plains of North Dakota, and the Badlands of South Dakota. Likewise practices that are used in the United States may be different from what is expected in other countries. Each area is unique, and using it in a way that preserves its quality depends on both your knowledge and your desire to do the proper thing. The more you practice minimum impact camping, the more you'll perfect your skills; the more you know about the plants, animals, soil, and water of an area, the better outdoor participant you'll become.

Minimum impact camping is a way of life, a philosophy of caring. Practicing minimum impact camping means that you will leave an area just as you found it or better. Certainly, concerned citizens understand the need to accept responsibility for their actions. If you don't know the best minimum impact practices for a given area, ask someone who does. The important thing is that you care and try to learn more about these skills as you progress. When your skills are sharply honed, you can then turn from student to teacher and teach minimum impact skills to others who are just as eager to learn as you are to teach.

What should you do? Consider the following ideas, which will make your effect on natural resources as minimal as possible.

Litter

In dealing with litter, follow two simple rules:

- Leave at home as much as you can of what you do need and all of what you don't need.

- If you must take something with you, remember that you must carry it home again.

Helpful Hints

If you carry something in, carry it out again.

- For a day hike, peel the oranges before you leave home, wrap them in plastic, and take the plastic back home with you at the end of the trip.

- For an overnight trip, leave at home much of the packaging of foodstuffs (cardboard, boxes, cellophane).

- When you're outdoors, package whatever trash you still have so that you can take it back home. Trash cans and dumpsters are appropriate places to dispose of trash; forests, streams, prairies, and deserts are not. Deer and wild rodents may eat a few discarded apple cores, but banana, orange, and melon peels don't decompose easily; they rot, smell bad, gather flies, and generally attract all kinds of problems.

- If you find litter from another group, do your part and pick it up and carry it out.

Campsites

In the past, many people commonly camped together at one site. Today, large groups of people camping in one place can ruin the quality of the environment and surpass the carrying capacity leading to damage of the environment. Large groups are noisier and scare away much of the wildlife. Parks or forest service personnel typically determine the number of people allowed at a site. Some areas may be designated for only four or five participants, while others might be set aside for larger groups. In the backcountry, some areas might be designated for only a few people within a certain area. Remember to research quotas before planning an outing with your group.

Helpful Hints

- If camping in an area with non-designated sites, spread the participants into smaller groups approximately 100 yards apart so that they'll have a minimum impact on each portion of the site.

- If camping in an area with designated sites, spread the group out to different sites to meet the approved number of participants per site.

- Take a smaller group on the outing.

- Camp at least 200 feet away from a stream, pond, or lake.

- At a popular site, it's best to camp where other participants have camped rather than to camp on the edge of that area. Camping on a new site creates a larger, wider area of trampling and causes general environmental change.

- In an area that very few people have used before you, spread the participants out so that they'll have a minimal effect on this rarely used site.

• Before you leave a campsite, go over the area carefully to remove all traces of your visit. Leave the campsite in the same condition you found it — if not better.

Tent Sites

When selecting a tent site, look for an area that is relatively level and not sitting in a depressed area. Because most tents today come with waterproof floors or participants can also put tarps under conventional tents, the old technique of trenching (digging a trench to keep rain from running under the tent) is not appropriate today. Digging not only is a great deal of work but also causes irreversible damage to soil and plants. If using a tarp under the tent, be sure to roll the edges of the trap underneath so that rain water will flow under the tarp and not on top of it.

Minimum Impact Fact

Do not clear an area to place your tent (brushing aside things such as leaves and pine needles). Doing so shows impact to the area, and most leaves and pine needles will serve as a cushion underneath the tent. Removing falling branches is permissible.

Toilets

What about making a toilet in the outdoors? Chapter 4, "Being Safe," addresses this subject in detail; you may, however, consider the following minimum impact practices:

• The first rule in relieving yourself outdoors is to use an existing toilet if one is available.

• If you will be camping in an area where toilets are not available, dispose of used toilet paper and other hygiene products in plastic bags (carry it in, carry it out); you can dispose of the bags and their contents when you get home.

Helpful Hint

Wet wipe products or pocket tissues are good to use as they are easy to carry and not bulky. Remember to carry out what you carry in.

• Consider using natural toilet paper, including both living and nonliving substances. Be careful what you choose; know your environment and its poisonous and bristly plants. Never disturb an entire plant by stripping all its leaves. Recently fallen soft leaves work well; snow is shocking, but it also works well. Be sure not to disturb the area by removing bunches of leaves and lots of rocks; choose your natural toilet paper carefully.

Washing

The goal in washing is to accomplish the task with as little effect on the environment as possible. When you're washing dishes or bathing, you don't need an entire lake, stream, or river, only clean water and a place to pour the dirty water. Be sure to use biodegradable soap. For more information on washing dishes refer to chapter 6, "Putting It on Your Plate."

Trails

Footsteps alone cause compaction and erosion, so take precautions to have minimal impact on a trail. Use designated trails. When traveling in the backcountry, which usually doesn't have designated trails, stay on rock or snow and spread out so that you don't all walk over the same area.

Helpful Hints

- Wear proper footwear that will help to minimize effects on both the earth and your feet.

- Do not cut across switchbacks (sharp curves in a trail are designed to keep water from rushing down and causing erosion). Using this shortcut can leave trails that become watercourses, causing serious erosion problems.

- If possible avoid hiking on muddy trails and restrain yourself from hiking on the shoulder of a muddy trail to keep your footwear clean and dry. Expect to get your shoes dirty.

Plants

Many plant species can be found when hiking through an area, and participants will want to examine them, particularly if they are unique.

ACA File Photo

Helpful Hints

- Leave plants as you find them. If you want to examine a soft leaf or petal, touch it gently instead of picking it; the sensation will be the same, and the plant will stand a better chance of surviving the ordeal.

- Bring along a plant ID book to help you identify what you are looking at.

- In many states, picking wildflowers is illegal. In any case, picking wildflowers often causes them to not reseed or reproduce. They don't last long if picked and are essential in providing nutrients back to the soil. Many wildflowers have short lives even if they're left alone.

Fires

A campfire is a beloved indispensable camping tradition. Minimum impact camping, however, means that we no longer build campfires to sit around in the evening and instead look to alternative heat sources to meet our outdoor needs.

Public wilderness and backcountry areas rarely allow fires. Repeated wood gathering depletes ground cover, fire rings take away from the natural setting, and unattended fires or poorly tended fires can lead to wildfires. When campfires are allowed, they are usually restricted to lower elevations (under 4000 feet) or to drive-in campgrounds with designated sites and fire containment devices.

Although some private lands and camps allow fires for cooking, the main purpose of building campfires today is for survival. At times, you may need a fire for an emergency signal or to warm a hypothermia victim. As you plan your outdoor experience, keep minimum impact principles in mind. See chapter 6, "Putting It on Your Plate," for specifics on how to build a campfire.

The Human Factor

Besides caring for the environment, minimum impact camping means leaving minimal impact on other campers and vice versa. Things that often annoy others include large crowds, people camping too close to them, noisy campers, dogs that bark or bound into other campsites, and loud music. Even certain colors of tents or tarps such as bright orange and pink may annoy those who camp to get away from it all. Bright colors do not blend into the background and show a "visual pollution." Be considerate when camping near or in the vicinity of other outdoor enthusiasts.

Just as you and your group have the potential to affect other groups, others might also affect your trip. You may need to alter your plans in the event another individual or group is in the same area and is too loud, or is behaving in a way that creates a negative experience or compromises the safety of your group. In such an event, be polite, keep your group together, minimize any conversation with the other party, and move away from the area, the group, or individual as soon as possible. Report any suspicious or threatening behavior to the local land manager or law enforcement. Remember that safety comes first!

Before you step out the door, plan your trip to reduce your impact on the environment. Minimal impact camping makes a better environment for everyone.

Risk Management: Planning for Survival

Every outdoor pursuit comes with some element of risk. Whether you are climbing a mountain, fording a stream, or hiking along a path, risk is inherent in all that we do. Be prepared for those unexpected incidences that can happen as part of an outdoor experience.

Simply defined, risk is the possibility of loss or injury. Risk management is defined as plans to identify, evaluate, reduce, prevent, or control the loss or injury. In other words, what procedures do you need to have in place to minimize risk on a trip? For example, if you want to hike with a group in the mountains, all participants must wear sturdy hiking shoes and travel with a buddy at all times. By implementing these two procedures, you can minimize the risk that someone will turn an ankle or get lost. Does this eliminate the risk? No, but it minimizes the risk so that participants are less likely to get injured or lost.

Why Plan for Survival?

Just as we plan for other parts of our outdoor excursions, we also need to plan for the unexpected, which may include survival in an outdoor environment. No one expects to be caught in a survival situation. When we think of survival, we have visions of overcoming storms in the Arctic, escaping from crocodiles, or surviving on a desert island while awaiting rescue. Others might think that survival means living off the land during a hike or canoe trip into uncharted wild areas. But most people don't plan to take such adventuresome vacations at any time. However, every year, hundreds of people find themselves unintentionally in a survival situation, whether they get lost from their group, ski down the wrong side of the mountain, or break down in the middle of the desert.

Survival situations can be caused by two factors — environmental and human. Environmental factors can include weather, fires, earthquakes, volcanic eruptions, floods, or landslides. These factors can happen unexpectedly and with no human intervention. For example, if you were driving your group down a deserted mountain pass and had to stop because of a rockslide across the road, several hours or days might pass before anyone knew you were there or had a chance to rescue you. This environmental factor resulted in a survival situation.

Human factors include relationships and decisions. Relationship factors can include how members of the group might get along. For example, one participant might get mad at another one, walk off from the group, and get lost. Decision factors might be deciding to hike when the weather forecast called for a blizzard in the mountains and you go anyway or didn't check the weather report. Whether a survival situation is caused by environmental or human factors, both preparation and a plan to minimize the risks are important.

Developing an Emergency Plan

Developing an emergency plan is an essential function before any outdoor activity whether a short day trip or an extensive backcountry trek. Emergency plans are just that, plans that are in place for you to follow in the event of an emergency. Some things that you need to consider are

- the location of the closest hospital;

- how you will contact help if someone is injured or ill;

- who will communicate with authorities, parents, and organization leaders and how they will do that;

- the exit routes out of an area in the event of a flood or fire;

- the procedure to follow if a participant or leader is lost and missing;

- who will stay with a group if there is an accident or illness;

- whether you called local authorities to let them know you would be in the area; and

- whether you have all health forms with you.

All these considerations are important components of an emergency plan. An emergency plan should be in place well before you leave on your trip and should also be filed with someone from your organization or someone who is not part of the trip.

What Does It Take to Be a Survivor?

Essential to survival is the will to live. People who want to live don't give up trying; they keep on planning and working to survive. Related to will to live is preparation — having planned what to do if something happens and what supplies would be needed. As part of your risk management, think about what could happen, and plan for all reasonable emergencies. Consider the following when planning for survival.

Protect yourself and others from extreme temperatures. Maintaining body heat or keeping the body from overheating is the first thing to consider when you plan for survival. The internal (core) temperature of most people is about 98.6°F. If the core temperature rises above 103°F or falls below 95°F, serious problems can occur. For that reason, you need adequate clothing and shelter. Pack additional clothing and wear layers so that you can remove layers as needed should it get warm or hot.

Have drinking water available. It doesn't take much to dehydrate. Even when resting, people must replace the water they lose through perspiration, respiration, and urination. When they're exercising, people need even more water; for example, a hiker needs three to four quarts per day just to prevent dehydration. A person at rest may die of dehydration after three days of going without water. Water is preferable, but sports drinks are also good to use. Be aware that soda and juices contain sugar, which can dehydrate you further.

When you are traveling on trail and away from home, consider your liquid needs and water availability. Will you be hiking in the heat? Will there be enough potable (suitable for drinking) water along the trail? Can you carry enough water to make it to a place where there is potable water? Be sure to assess your water supply before heading out on any outdoor excursion, and make sure everyone in your group is adequately prepared.

Keep high-energy foods on hand. Food can seem to be more important than water; however, you can go longer without food (up to three weeks) than you can without water. Even though you can survive longer without food, it is always good to be prepared with additional supplies on hand.

High-energy foods that don't require cooking, such as dried fruit, nuts, chocolate, and cheese are good choices and can fit easily into a pack. Cold cereal, particularly homemade or purchased granola, is good to snack on, and don't forget about GORP (Good Old-fashioned Raisins and Peanuts, which can include marshmallows, chocolate chips, M&Ms, or other snacks you might want to throw in).

Today, taking along a cell phone is a good safety precaution. Although some cell phones won't work in more remote areas, it is always good to have on hand in the event of an emergency.

In addition to the will to live, protection from extreme weather and the availability of adequate drinking water and high-energy foods are required for basic survival. There really isn't any good reason for anyone not to be prepared for emergencies outdoors; it just takes common sense and wise planning.

In a survival situation remember the following acronym: STOP!

Stop (don't panic),

Think (about what you're going to do, what you need, and what you have),

Observe (the situation; what you need to do in a hurry; and how to stay where you are, using what is available nearby),

Plan (what you'll do, how you'll do it, when you'll do it, and why you'll do it).

As the leader, it is up to you to keep a cool and level head and take one thing at a time. Remember that the most important thing is that everyone is safe.

Staying Found

Besides making it through bad weather, the survival situation that worries most parents and participants is getting lost, particularly if they have never been in an outdoor environment before. People who get lost on an outdoor excursion are lost not only to themselves but also to those who will soon start looking for them.

Helpful Hints

- Plan where you'll be going, and find out as much as possible about the area. Will there be snow on the trail? Is the water unusually high or low? Has the trail been rerouted or washed away?

- Make a list of the equipment you'll need and check off each item as you pack it.

- Tell someone where you're going, were the place is, and when you plan to return. And then stick to your plan! Be sure to let the person you told know when you return.

- File a trip plan, including driving routes and anticipated times of arrival, with the sponsoring agency.

- Make sure that everyone in the group also knows where the group is going; don't be the only one with the plan. If something should happen to you, someone else will need to take over.

- Plan for emergency exits. Plan which trails and other escape routes to take if there is a forest fire, an extremely bad storm, or a medical emergency that requires you to leave the area in a hurry.

- Take along enough emergency equipment so that if you're lost or injured, you can stay warm, dry, and comfortable for at least 24 hours.

- Travel in a group. A youth group should plan on a ratio of one leader for every eight participants, plus one extra.

- Never wander away from the group alone. Count in an obvious manner to see that all participants are present before the group starts off again.

- When someone leaves the group for toilet purposes, that person should be sure he or she knows how to return.

- No one should go out of earshot of the group.

- Use the buddy system and make sure that all members of the group know where they are going. Give them a designated time to return.

- All participants must be able to take some responsibility for themselves. If some members of the group have learning, vision, or hearing impairments, buddies or leaders who can see, hear, and observe where they are going should accompany those people. Being aware of where the group is at all times and staying together are keys to staying found.

Surviving Being Lost

Even though you have planned how to stay found, everyone needs to know how to survive being lost. What happens if someone becomes confused and strays away from the group, or if the group makes a faulty decision and loses the trail? How can other people find you?

Helpful Hints

If you become lost:

- STAY WHERE YOU ARE! Remain in one place, keep warm and dry, and make yourself visible. If you move from place to place, you may move away from seekers and into areas where they've already finished looking for you.

- If you hear people, use your whistle or call to them.

- At night, you might light a small fire for comfort. Search parties usually don't look at night so get some sleep. Find or build a shelter and remember that animals may be attracted to food, so keep all foodstuffs away from yourself and from the group. If you're with your buddy or in a group, play games such as Twenty Questions, tell jokes, or sing songs.

Remember that there are two different types of emergency "survival" situations: those caused by environmental factors and those caused by human factors. You can prepare for the environmental factors; leaders and participants alike have the responsibility to prevent situations caused by human error.

Planning for emergencies is a prerequisite for any leader. No leader should ever neglect to take precautions because an emergency didn't occur last time and doesn't seem likely to occur this time. Be firm to ensure that the participants follow proper precautions.

You can prepare for emergencies by planning for adequate shelter, adequate protection from the weather, adequate liquids, and adequate high-energy foods. Following the STOP formula, staying in one place if you're lost, and being sure that someone knows where to look for you if you don't get back on time are sure ways to help you survive in the outdoors.

Planning

One of the most effective ways to provide a sense of ownership with any outdoor activity is to involve the group in the decision making. What are their opinions? What would they like to do? How much time would they like to spend? What would they like to eat? Where would they like to stay? Ideally they should plan the project with you; however, sometimes many of these details are already in place, especially when reservations or permits are required. Nevertheless, allow the group members to make a few of the decisions about their outdoor activity such as planning for what to do after they reach their destination and deciding the kind of food they would like to have. Early participation in the decision-making process will allow the participants to "buy in" to the process, which will make the activity a more pleasant opportunity for all involved.

Group Involvement in Planning

Planning as a group helps to establish a working relationship and provides a systematic approach, providing order, clarity, and purpose to the task. The project leader has the responsibility to facilitate the discussion by encouraging and giving group members opportunities to participate. Participation in the group discussion requires involvement, motivation to contribute, and acceptance of responsibility for one's actions. Keep in mind that some participants may be reluctant to take part because they are unfamiliar with the project or the environment or they may just be shy.

Making Decisions

Many decisions need to be made before you head off on your outdoor adventure. Use the template in appendix D to help the group plan the outdoor activity. Group members who help to set their own rules and are a part of what they are going to be doing will be more likely to follow the rules, help hold their group accountable, and have a sense of pride and accomplishment to the success of the trip.

The group will need to address the following questions.

- Why is the group doing this? What is the purpose or the intent of the activity? Why does the group want to go? If you have group members who aren't as gung ho as you would like, who say they are going because they have to go, help them develop some short-term goals to help achieve success with the activity.

- When and where is the group going? The group needs to determine the time to do the project. Group readiness, weather, time of year, and the physical attractions of the area will all determine where the group would like to go. Remember to allow enough time from the decision to go to the actual time of the trip. It is important to have enough preparation time to allow for getting ready to go, planning your route, getting and packing your food and equipment, determining methods of transportation, raising funds for your event if that is required, getting in touch with the Resource Manager, and completing other project planning.

- How long will the group stay? The group needs to decide how long the activity will be. This could be as short as a day to a week-long backcountry trip. Remember to include transportation time, project time, and recreational time.

- What will the group do at the location? Going back to the "why" of the group project will help you focus on what needs to be done while at the location site. Consider what time is needed for specific activities such as hiking, swimming, or picnicking.

- How many adults need to go and who will that be? At least two adults should accompany any group. If there are more than a dozen children or youth in a group, include at least one adult for every six to eight additional participants. The advantage to having more than one adult in the group is that should an emergency arise or an adult become incapacitated, another adult will be there to go for help or to assist the rest of the group.

One of the adults in the group must be first aid and CPR certified. If you are planning skilled activities, someone who has been trained and certified for that activity and the equipment being used should be present. For example, when planning any type of water-related recreational activity such as boating, canoeing, or swimming, an individual in the group who is certified as a lifeguard from a certifying body (American Red Cross, YMCA, Boy Scouts, Ellis and Associates, etc.) should accompany the group.

Transportation

Transportation is another consideration. Group members may be able to reach local destinations by walking. In urban areas, public transportation may be the answer. Depending on the size of the group, you can drive cars or vans; however, leasing a bus for the duration of the project may be appropriate. If you do lease a bus or arrive (especially if it is a long distance) by train or plane, what transportation will you need to have at your destination? If you initially take a bus, will you need additional modes of transportation such as bikes or canoes to get around the area? These are some of the things to keep in mind as you plan your transportation.

Design a practical transportation plan with your group. Will vehicles be available when and where they are needed? Do you need a vehicle to drop your group off and then pick it up on the other end of the hike, canoe, or bike ride? The vehicles used should be designed for carrying passengers and have the appropriate number of seat belts for the total number of people in the group. You should be assured that the vehicles are in good condition and have had a recent safety check. If the group is going by car, van, or bus, the driver of each vehicle must be appropriately licensed and insured and each vehicle must be safe. If drivers are required, you need to determine who they will be and whether they need a special license to drive.

Equipment

The equipment you'll need for outdoor living depends on how far you'll be going from home base or another place that offers shelter, water, heat, and emergency help. When you choose equipment, always consider the situation and all possible variations. The weather, the temperature, the season, the participants' stress and activity levels, their size and age, their experience, the distance and method of travel, the possible hazards, and group interactions all play a part in planning appropriate equipment.

Look at base-site equipment first. If your base site is a camping area in a state forest, you'll need comfortable, sturdy clothes that are dark in color so they won't show evidence of soil, charcoal, or dirt. In warmer climates, gray-colored clothing is a better choice to reduce the site of dirt soil and to keep you cooler in the heat of the sun. Long pants, t-shirts, sweatshirts, court or athletic shoes, hiking boots, socks, and a windbreaker may be all you'll need at base camp as long as you can reach shelter within a few minutes. If you are only out for a day trip, your base site might be the van in the parking lot of a county park, and most of the equipment you will need for the day will be stored in your pack. Find out where the group can go for shelter from the elements or to get additional clothing, raincoats, or jackets if the weather changes and becomes cold or rainy.

On a trip away from your base site, you must carry everything that you'll need; it won't be possible to return to base or go to a store for additional equipment. Keep in mind the activities you will be doing while away from your base site. If the group is planning on wading across a stream, does everyone have water shoes to protect their feet in the water? Items you need on a short duration trip such as a day hike need to be lightweight, compact, and easy to carry.

The Ten Essentials

1. Extra clothing and shelter. Include items that can serve as shelter as well as protection from cold, dampness, or heat.

2. Extra water. Take along an extra quart of water (two quarts if you're in the desert) in addition to your regular supply. Keep refilling the canteen whenever you can.

3. Extra food. Appropriate extra foods include things such as GORP and nutrition or granola bars. A list of appropriate high-energy extra foods is provided in chapter 6, "Putting It on Your Plate."

4. A pocketknife. Bring a pocketknife in good working condition.

5. A flashlight with extra batteries and bulb. Reverse one of the batteries in your flashlight; in that way, it won't accidentally get turned on inside the pack, wearing the batteries down. Reversing both batteries will drain them.

6. Matches and fire starter. Carry matches in a waterproof container. Waterproof matches and containers can be purchased at your local outdoor store, or empty film canisters work exceptionally well and are small enough for storage. Also pack some type of fire starter; a list can be found in chapter 6, "Putting It on Your Plate."

7. Map and compass. You should know how to use these two essential pieces of equipment. Outdoor travelers must know which direction they came from and in which direction they are traveling. A GPS (Global Positioning System) is also an added value if you have one.

8. Sun protection. A hat with a brim and sunscreen with at least an SPF (Sun Protection Factor) of 15 as well as long pants and long sleeves are also useful in protecting from the sun (depending on climate and environment). Carry a pair of sunglasses for use when the sun is bright, and don't forget lip protection, which can have sunscreen in it.

9. First aid kit. All outdoor travelers should have access to a complete first aid kit. It should be carried and administered by the leader or designated first aid person when in a group. Adults can carry their own prescriptions, but be aware of all medication taken by any member of the group. Any youth participants should give his or her personal medication to the leader, who can then dispense it properly. If you dispense medication on a trip, keep a log of the person you gave the medication to, the type of medication, the dosage, and the time you gave it.

10. Optional items (toilet paper, whistle, or mirror). Many people also carry folded toilet paper, a whistle, and/or a mirror along with the rest of the equipment. Use a whistle or mirror as an emergency signal only; never use it unless you're lost or need help. If you use any toilet paper while in the outdoors, carry it out and dispose of it properly.

Carry enough equipment to keep yourself warm and dry (or cool and dry) for at least 24 hours in the event you get lost or stuck. It may take that long or even longer for help to arrive, but at least you are prepared with the right gear.

Gear for Outdoor Activities

Planning outdoor activities involves organizing tools and equipment. Outdoor equipment must be lightweight, sturdy, and compact — and necessary. The novice will bring lots of extra gear tied to his or her pack, banging, clanging, and jolting on the walk down the trail, and a younger novice might bring a teddy bear or pillow on an overnight.

Clothing and Shelter Equipment

When it comes to clothing and shelter, campers, hikers, canoeists, and most other outdoor enthusiasts seem to have their own vocabulary. Like musicians, athletes, and dancers, outdoor experts talk about things that those who aren't part of the group may not understand — polypro, Goretex, Hollofill, Cordura, parkas, anoraks, Montagna, gaiters, ragg, and other strange-sounding items. The novice may find these names quite foreign, and the dictionary may not list them. This book discusses only those things that outdoors people commonly use. Materials are changing so rapidly that the many man-made fabrics will be called "synthetics" here. Put together a clothing and equipment list (including the ten essential items) for the members of your group so that they can check off the supplies as they pack.

Choosing Clothing Material

All good things come in threes! When choosing clothing material, prepare your clothes in three different layers. The first layer closest to your skin is a moisture control layer. This layer wicks (takes away) moisture from your body and absorbs it into the material. The second layer should be an insulating layer, designed to keep your body warm. The third layer or the outer layer is a weatherproofing layer designed to keep out wind and rain. The combination of these three layers will allow you to remove clothes when you are too warm and conversely add layers as you get colder.

Cotton

Cotton is the choice of most campers in the summertime because it holds moisture, which helps keep you cool in the summer; the breeze that blows over your damp t-shirt evaporates the moisture, taking your body heat with it. Conversely, cotton will not keep you warm in the winter or during wet weather.

Cotton underwear, bandannas, and shirts are particularly good for summer wear. Chamois and flannel are heavy cotton and are comfortable when the weather is a bit chilly and these materials are kept dry.

Wool

Wool keeps you warm in cold weather. Wool clothing will insulate you from cold wind if you cover it with a windproof jacket. Unlike cotton, wool retains some of its insulating ability when it's wet, but not when it's matted with perspiration and body oils. On the downside, wool takes a long time to dry.

Second-hand stores are good sources of extra-large heavy wool sweaters. Function over fashion is the rule here. Forget about a fancy style; find something that will keep you warm.

Synthetics

Synthetics are materials made from something other than plants or animals. Polypropylene fiber (commonly called "polypro") is one of the most popular synthetic fabrics and may keep you warm when it's wet. Polypro wicks moisture away from your body and is recommended for sock liners (the pair next to your feet) and for long underwear worn during strenuous exercise, such as cross-country skiing.

Fleece is a synthetic material that is most popular among outdoor enthusiasts. The material is warm, even when wet; dries rapidly; and is half the weight of wool material. You do need to be careful when around an open fire however, as this material tends to melt rather than burn.

Nylon, which is another synthetic, makes wonderful windproof clothes. Nylon is not waterproof unless it is coated with a waterproof substance, but it really does a good job in repelling the wind.

Sleeping bags may be insulated with synthetics such as Polarguard, Hollofill, or Qualofill. These materials are easy to launder, retain much of their insulating qualities when they're wet, and dry fairly rapidly.

Goretex is a patented material that is both breathable and waterproof. (Rain can't penetrate the material, but perspiration can.) The micropore material allows the body to "breathe" so that the moisture does not accumulate inside the coat or boots.

Down

Pound for pound, down (the fluffy feathers from geese or ducks) is the warmest insulation available and is used in sleeping bags and other clothing. Down does not provide much insulation when wet and takes a long time to dry. Down sleeping bags are useful where the temperature falls below freezing, but be warned that they can be expensive to purchase. A down vest under a wind layer can be a warm combination. It is a little warmer than fleece but also a little bulkier.

Type of Clothing

The type of clothing you'll need depends on the area and the season. Remember to dress for the weather and be prepared in case of weather changes. In the summer, you might want to stick to cotton unless you're traveling in those parts of the United States that are noted for cold nights and occasional summer snow, such as high elevations and northern areas. In the winter, prepare for cold, damp, and wet weather, particularly if you are in colder ranges.

Warm weather clothing includes:

- t-shirts,

- shorts,

- fleece sweater or sweatshirt,

- windbreaker,

- pants to put on when the weather gets cooler (convertible pants, which have zip-off legs that convert to shorts, are popular today), and

- brimmed hat.

During cold weather, carry several layers of clothing that you can add or remove one at a time when the temperature changes including:

- long sleeve t-shirt;

- sweater, sweatshirt, or fleece pullover;

- wool or synthetic jacket;

- wind- or waterproof jacket or parka;

- stocking or wool cap;

- long underwear;

- pants; and

- wind- or weatherproof outer shell.

Helpful Hint

Denim jeans can get heavy when they're wet. As the moisture evaporates, you can become very cold and contract hypothermia. If the only pants you have are denim, be sure to have rain pants that you can put on before the jeans get wet.

Rainwear

Rainwear is an important piece of equipment whether you are traveling in hot or cold weather. Be aware of the difference between water repellent and waterproof. Water repellent jackets do not completely keep moisture out and are good for light rain or snow but become wet in heavier precipitation. Waterproof clothing, if you have it, is the best defense against the wet weather and does not allow water to absorb into the material.

Helpful Hint

Typically clothing you wear in the outdoors should blend in with the environment. Bright colors can not only attract unwanted insects but can also be offensive to other travelers looking for a natural experience. However, if you'll be traveling in an area where hunting is permitted, be sure to wear bright clothing such as red or blaze orange so that hunters can identify you.

ACA File Photo

Footwear

With nearly all outdoor activities, the most important part of your body is your feet, which must carry you to and from your destination. Your feet must carry your weight plus the weight of your pack or load. You may encounter rough spots, stones, sand, brambles, hills, rough terrain, and many other things where you will need appropriate shoes.

Safety Tip

Walking in wet shoes can cause blisters.

Use the following suggestions as a guideline when selecting footwear and preparing for your trip:

- Consider how well your shoes or boots support your feet and ankles.

- Condition your feet and break in your shoes. Walk, wearing the shoes or boots in which you'll be hiking, before you go out on the hike.

- Make sure footwear is appropriate for the terrain. Sandals are not a good footwear choice when hiking through the woods. Athletic shoes, particularly ones with thick soles, may be fine for short trips on fairly soft and even ground.

- Stop any pain before it gets worse, either at home or on the trail. Remove your shoes and take care of high spots (where boots rub) or other areas of concern. Use a band-aid or moleskin on sensitive areas before they become blistered.

- Take an old pair of lightweight athletic shoes to use for wading or just walking around the campsite for an overnight trip.

- Sandals with adjustable synthetic hook and loop straps, and molded rubber soles, are good for canoeing, beaches, or other water activities.

- Hiking boots are necessary for hiking above 5000 feet in the Rockies, Cascades, Sierras, and other mountain ranges where there are many rough rocks and snow may be on the trail.

- Consider the activities and terrain before you select your own footwear or recommend any to other people. Find out what is recommended for your area and the intended use by asking other hikers, knowledgeable leaders, and sportinggoods–store personnel.

- When you try on a pair of boots, wear the type of socks and liners that you plan to wear on the trail. A thin inner pair should wick the perspiration away to the outside socks, and the outside socks serve as an insulator and cushion.

Helpful Hint

If your feet are cold, put on a hat. Most of the body's heat escapes through the head.

Tents and Other Shelters

Tents and tarps are available in many sizes, shapes, fabrics, and weights. When considering tents, your group can discuss where and how you will be traveling, for how long, and in what season. It's possible to have a tent that will sleep anywhere from one to eight people. A poncho will make a small shelter for one person in a pinch.

Making a Tarp Tent

You can use a tarp with grommets or make an excellent tarp tent from a 9-foot by 12-foot piece of 4- to 6-mil polyethylene. This inexpensive material usually comes in black or white and is available at most hardware stores.

Stretch the material out on the ground and mark the tie-down spots with a waterproof marker or plastic tape in a contrasting color on the tarp. When you get to your campsite, attach tie-downs to the seven appropriately marked spots. To attach tie-downs, use small round pinecones or stones.

You will also need seven nylon cords, each about 3 feet long. Put a pinecone under a tie-down spot and wrap part of one nylon cord around the tie-down spot so that it looks like you're holding the pinecone inside (like you are wrapping a piece of candy in cellophane). Secure it with a clove hitch or a double half-hitch. (Chapter 7, "Tools and Ties," discusses how to tie knots.) The loose end of the cord will attach to a tent stake.

To pitch the tarp tent, follow these steps:

- Tie the center of the front to a tree at a point about 5 feet from the ground (about chin level for an adult).

- Stretch the back out to meet the ground, and secure it to the tent stake at the tie-down spots (3 feet in from each corner).

- Adjust the front corners as desired and stake them down.

- Adjust the sides to tighten the tent and stake them down.

- Tuck the back corners under. The corners make a good ground cloth for your gear and serve to tighten the back of the tent.

This tarp tent doesn't cost much and is very lightweight. Up to four youngsters can sleep in it easily, and even four large adults can squeeze into it in a pinch. If you just need shelter from the wind or a light rain, you can make a tarp tent from a tarp with grommets. String a line between two trees at a height of about one third the length of the tarp. Fold the tarp over the line and spread the sides out and stake down. If you have a longer tarp you can fold the tarp in thirds and put one third on the ground to provide the ground cloth. The ends of this tent are open so it is important to be sure to position the tent so that the wind and/or rain hits the side of the tent and not the end.

Synthetic Tents

Most outdoor enthusiasts today carry tents made of lightweight synthetic materials. Canvas tents, common in many youth camps for semi-permanent housing, are heavy and leak when they're subjected to long rains; they're also hard to keep clean and are likely to mildew and rot if not cleaned or dried appropriately.

Tents are usually manufactured from lightweight nylon. A good tent will have a waterproof floor and waterproof "rain fly" that covers breathable lightweight nylon tops and sides. If the top is made of uncoated material, it will leak; if the top is made of coated material, it will sweat and drip condensation on the occupants. Rain flies serve as water barriers and insulators,

Tents come in various shapes and sizes. Two of the most popular shapes are A-Frame and Dome tents.

permitting moisture to escape through the top of the tent and dissipate into the air. Flies should be long enough to cover all the uncoated areas of the tent so that no moisture can seep in. Most tents have fiberglass poles that fit together to form a dome and to stretch the fabric tight across a frame.

Pitch the tent according to the instructions provided by the manufacturer. Practice at home (even with groups) before you are on the trail or in the dark.

Choosing the size and weight of your tent will depend on when you are traveling (warmer or cooler months) and also how many people will be sharing it with you. Tents are generally classified by sleeping capacity and can range from single person tents to bigger family tents. Use the following as a guide to assist you when selecting a tent.

- Single-person tents are small with enough room for one person and not much more.

- One- to two-person tents provide enough shelter for one person with a little room to spare or can fit two people snugly.

- Two-person tents will sleep two and are the most popular backpacking tent among outdoor enthusiasts. They come with various features, so do your homework and pick one that works the best for you.

- Two- to three-person tents fit two people relatively well with a little room to spare. Generally they are taller and wider than two-person tents, so a third person can fit, but it is tight.

- Three-person tents work well for three people but do pack a little more weight due to additional material.

- Four-person tents provide enough room for four but generally weigh a little bit more. These tents are ideal for campground camping if you don't have to hike too far but are not suggested for smaller participants who would struggle with the additional weight. For summer camp programs and other organizations that would do camping on site or close to their home base, these tents are ideal for larger groups such as a scout troop or cabin that might be taking an overnight.

- Family tents are huge tents, which use sturdy thick poles and heavier material than smaller tents. Because these tents are heavier to transport and are designed to be used with many people, their best use is served in campground or car camping.

Helpful Hints

- All tents should be waterproof, sturdy enough to withstand wind and hard rain, and easy to pitch and pack.

- Tents should be in dark unobtrusive colors (see the material on psychological carrying capacity earlier in this chapter).

- Match your tent to the kind of environment in which you plan to travel: the season, the presence of mosquitoes, and the possibility of rain, wind, or snow.

- If your tent does not have a waterproof floor, be sure to carry along a ground tarp to place underneath. The ground tarp should be slightly smaller than the dimension of the tent floor. This will help prevent moisture from being absorbed into the floor and any rainwater from coming into your tent.

- When packing up tents, wrap all the hardware in the tent before rolling and putting it in its bag. This helps to prevent equipment loss so that you know where everything is and don't have to hunt for it.

Caring for Your Tent

Proper care of your tent is very important for long-lasting use. The number one rule in caring for your tent is to make sure that it is dry before you pack it. Packing a wet tent away is a surefire invitation for mildew to grow, which will eventually eat away at the fabric. Synthetic tents tend to dry quickly; however, if you have to take down a tent in wet weather, be sure to dry it out later (including the bag you packed it in and any rope that will be packed with it). You can set it up to dry at home in your backyard or even spread it out inside so all sides and the floor can dry thoroughly.

Sleeping Bags

Sleeping bags come in many shapes, designs, weights, and materials. The type of bag you select depends on where you will be going, how you will be traveling, how often you'll use it, and how much you want to spend. Before you select a sleeping bag or recommend one to others, review the material on synthetics and down earlier in this chapter.

Many sleeping bags are made of synthetic material and have a heat rating. For example, a sleeping bag that is made for three seasons (spring, summer, and fall) may have a rating of above 35°F, while a sleeping bag made for the winter might have a rating between -10°F to +35°F. The type of camping you will be doing will determine the kind of bag you buy.

Sleeping bags come in two basic styles, rectangular and mummy. Rectangular bags are roomier, heavier, and bulkier than the other shapes. These bags are less efficient in cold weather because the large pocket of air around the feet is hard for the body to heat. Mummy bags are smaller, easier to pack, and lighter in weight than rectangular bags. These bags are narrow at the foot and wide at the shoulders,

Most people wear modified sleeping garments in sleeping bags. Clean t-shirts used just for sleeping are fine in warm weather; long underwear and clean socks are a good choice in colder regions. Sleepwear must be different from the clothes you wear during the day because these garments are likely to be damp from perspiration and won't keep you warm.

Helpful Hint

If your sleeping bag does not have a bag or ties to secure it when rolled or stuffed, a stuff bag or compression bag may be helpful. Roll your sleeping clothes in with the bag and you won't have trouble finding them.

Sleeping Pads

In the past, campers slept on the hard ground, made little indentations in the sand or soil for their hips and shoulders, or made beds out of boughs. But today, the ground is too hard for most people, indentations ruin the land, and cutting boughs to make a soft bed is one of the fastest ways to destroy the environment.

If you don't want to sleep on the ground, you can take a sleeping pad with you. Sleeping pads are usually only 48 inches long — just long enough to keep the shoulders and hips comfortable. Three-quarter-length pads are economical and can be used from year to year. Most pads are foam or inflatable (some are even self-inflating), and many have a waterproof cover. Sleeping pads not only make sleeping more comfortable but also provide insulation to keep you warmer and drier.

Cooking Gear

For an overnight trip, you'll need a variety of cooking utensils and supplies. A complete list of these items appears in chapter 6, "Putting It on Your Plate."

Packs

Packs for hiking and other non-motorized travel come in two different forms, day packs and multiday packs. The type and duration of your trip will determine which pack you use, depending on how much equipment and supplies you will need.

Choosing a Pack

Choosing a pack whether for personal or group use requires careful consideration. You can't expect the first pack you see to fit properly. As an individual, you can choose your pack based on your personal preference and expectations of the pack and the trips you will be taking. If, however, you are purchasing equipment for a variety of people, or if you are a youth organization, a camp program, an environmental or adventure program that provides equipment for your participants, there are several things to keep in mind.

Day Packs

Day packs are carried on the back and held in place by two shoulder straps. Useful day packs are waterproof and have one to three outside pockets for extra clothing, water, food, rain gear, and other essentials. You can use a large day pack for a one-night trip, but you'll rarely have room for a sleeping bag, tent, stove, sleeping pad, and extra food.

Some people who make long backpack trips add a lightweight day pack or belt pack to their load for short hikes away from their overnight sites. Many mountain climbers add heavier, larger day packs to their backpacks to carry their climbing gear and emergency supplies in case they are stranded on the mountain.

Day packs come in sizes ranging from approximately 12 inches x 10 inches x 8 inches to 22 inches x 14 inches x 13 inches. Their capacity may be from around 1000 cubic inches to more than 3000 cubic inches. The smaller ones are adequate for most day hikers. Features to look for in day packs include pockets into which your water bottle will fit, adequate space for clothing and emergency supplies, and a place to carry your lunch.

Multiday Packs

For overnight trips, you'll need a multiday pack to carry your shelter, food, cooking equipment, clothing, and all the other supplies you'll need for living outdoors on the trail or along the river for one or more days and nights.

Multiday packs or frame packs can be either internal or external and come in sizes for men, women, and youth. One of the best reasons for using a frame pack is that the frame, with a hip belt, helps distribute the load over your hips, thus eliminating strain on your back. A hip belt is a necessity for holding the bag snug against your hips so that the load is distributed evenly and not just on your shoulders. Hip belts also prevent the pack from swaying and throwing you off balance.

Internal-frame packs are narrower than external-frame packs and have the support built right into the pack itself. An internal-frame pack fits closer to the body, forming to the body of the person who is wearing it. These packs permit more freedom of body movement than external frame packs. Typically they should be used for personal gear versus group or camp stock because they are not designed to carry the bulkier gear. Multiday packs can vary in size with smaller ones built for shorter duration trips and longer ones for extended trekking.

Who's better suited for an internal-frame pack?

• climbers

• skiers

• backpackers or cross-country hikers covering difficult or rough terrain

External-frame packs have the framing on the outside of the pack, are made from aluminum, and are padded with webbing to keep the frame from hitting the user's back, hips, and shoulders. External-frame packs are better for group settings such as camps or Scouts, where a variety of people might use the packs. Because the frame is external, it is more rigid and won't conform to the person who is using it.

Who's better suited for an external-frame pack?

• beginning hikers

• group participants where equipment is provided by one source

• hikers hauling heavy loads over easy to moderate trails and terrain

Size

Packs generally come in three sizes: small, medium, and large. The size of your participants may determine which size you purchase for your organization. Youth packs tend to be smaller and shorter. Packs for women have narrower shoulder straps, a smaller torso, and a smaller hip belt. If your participants are varied (children and adults), you might want to consider a mix of packs for your organization. If you have only youth participants, you might need to adjust your purchases to small and medium-sized packs. Realize that full-grown men probably use large packs. Be aware that some youth participants may be as big as an adult or smaller than their age group. Regardless of the size, some packs are made for overnight or short trips (approximately 2500 – 3700 cubic inches) and larger ones are available for longer treks of a week or more (3800 – 7000 cubic inches). Be sure to ask about the capacity of packs before you make a final selection.

Internal Versus External

Typically internal-frame packs are good for individual use because the internal frame tends to form to the shape of the user. If users are different every time, the internal-frame pack might not be comfortable for everyone. External-frame packs are better selections for organizations that provide equipment for their participants. External-frame packs remain rigid and do not conform to the body shape of the user. They also carry a lot more cargo.

Seasons

The season you travel in is also important in the selection of your pack. Packs come in specific sizes. The pack you choose for a week-long trek in the Outback of Australia would probably be smaller than the pack you would choose to hike in the middle of January in the White Mountains of Vermont. The amount of clothes and supplies will be greater in cooler climates.

Helpful Hint

Hydration packs (packs with a plastic bladder and long hose attached) already have a water system built into them to allow for easy drinking while on trail, bike, or other mode of transportation where your hands may not be free. Most hydration packs also have extra storage room for additional water bottles if necessary. If the trip you are planning requires greater amounts of water than normal, you might want to choose this pack.

Whichever pack you decide to use, keep in mind where you are going, for how long, and who will be using it.

ACA File Photo

Fitting a Pack

Be sure to fit all of your participants to the packs they will be using. A pack should fit like an extension of the body and should be comfortable when the user is walking. The size of the pack is very important. A pack should not extend above the head or below the buttocks, and the shoulder straps should wrap around, not gap at the shoulders. A pack that is too short or too long is very uncomfortable.

Keep the following in mind when fitting a pack with participants in your group:

Torso length measurement. Measuring the length of a participant's torso will help you identify the size of the pack to be used. To do so, measure the length from the vertebrae parallel to the top of the shoulder to the small of the back, even with the top of the hip bones.

Shoulder strap placement. The shoulder straps should fit comfortably but snugly without any gaps between the straps and your shoulders. The straps should be far enough apart so that they don't squeeze the skin but don't fall off the shoulders. The buckle straps should be far enough below the armpit so it won't chafe the skin.

Torso fit. The pack should fit properly if the weight of the pack is evenly distributed between the shoulders and the hips. Adjusting the shoulder straps will allow you to distribute the weight between the shoulders and the hips.

Chest strap. The chest strap should be positioned 2 inches below the collarbone. The chest strap does not need to be fastened at all times, but it is extremely helpful when hiking over rough territory.

Packs must be comfortable if the participants are to enjoy their excursion into the outdoors. When trying on different packs, a participant should ask these questions:

• Does it feel good to walk with it?

• Is it uncomfortable; does it pinch or bind or restrict my movement?

• Can I look up without hitting the back of my head on the top of the pack?

• Does it hit the back of my legs? Can I squat without losing circulation in my legs?

Packing the Pack

Heavy things should generally be at the bottom of the pack and as close to the body as possible. Items that won't be used during the day should also be at the bottom, as close together as possible. Pack clothing and other light gear around heavier items to keep them from shifting. Items that will be needed during the day should be packed near the top for easy access when on the trail. Many people prefer to pack personal items and clothes in smaller stuff bags.

Most modern packs are waterproof. If the pack is not waterproof or heavy precipitation is forecast, use a rain cover for the pack or open a large garbage bag on the inside of the pack and insert clothes, equipment, and other supplies. In this way, if the pack gets wet, clothes and other equipment will stay dry.

Sleeping bags that are strapped onto the bottom of a pack should have waterproof covers. If a cover is not available, a garbage bag will work as a good substitute; put the sleeping bag inside and tie the bag shut.

Each participant should have a small plastic bag (plastic grocery bags work well) in which to pack dirty clothes. Make sure that dirty clothes are dry and pack them away from food and clean clothes. Store eating and cooking tools together in a separate bag.

Have a discussion with others in your group about sharing equipment and how to pack things. No single way is best, but some ways are better than others. For example, you might not want to pack the crackers at the bottom of the bag and then place a bag of apples on them! Specifics on packing food are covered in chapter 6, "Putting It on Your Plate."

Pack Weight

How much weight is too much? The answer to that question depends on the age, size, and physical condition of each person. A good rule is to carry no more than 25 percent of your body weight. For example, a 100-pound camper in reasonably good physical condition should carry a maximum of 25 pounds of gear in a backpack. A 150-pound adult may be able to carry 40 to 50 pounds for some short trips; the pack gets lighter as the trip progresses and the food is eaten. Plan carefully so that the effort of carrying a pack doesn't ruin your trip. It takes a great deal of thought and skill to pack light.

Summary

Participants who are new to outdoor living skills need not go out and purchase all the latest and greatest equipment. As the leader, give your group members suggestions about what they can bring on their trip and the amounts. Some outdoor stores will also have equipment available for rent, so if someone would like to try equipment or needs it for a short duration, renting might be a good route to go.

Planning your outdoor living skills experiences requires planning for minimal effect on the environment and safety for the participants. Plan for risk and always ask yourself, "Is this the best plan or the safest way?" Minimum impact camping means using the land and water so that they remain in good condition. Safety means knowing how to survive in emergency situations and choosing and using appropriate supplies and equipment. You are well on your way to having a successful outdoor experience!

Being Safe

ACA File Photo

This chapter discusses safety issues. With any activity, the first thing you as a program leader need to ask yourself is "What is the safest way to do this?" As discussed in previous chapters, you need to think about many details when planning, preparing, and going on your trip, and safety is one of the biggest priorities. We will explore five specific topics in regard to safety: weather, drinking water, toilets, first aid, and animals, insects, and plants.

Related to all five topics are basic safety rules that every group should discuss and every participant should know and respect.

Safety Rules

- Use the buddy system. Participants (both children and adults) should always travel in pairs; in this way, everyone is accountable for someone.

- No one should leave the area where the group is without the leader's permission (even if you are an adult). The leader or another adult should always know where you are going.

- All participants should know their boundaries, where they can or can not go without a leader or proper supervision. For example, if participants wanted to go to the waterfront for swimming, a lifeguard would have to be present.

- Leaders should always be the first and last in line. Keep your group between the two. Traveling in this way there is less of a chance someone from your group will get separated. A responsible adult or youth leader (someone who may not be leading the trip out) can also be the last in line as long as he or she understands that the task is to keep the group in front of him or her.

- The group should stop for frequent water breaks (particularly if it is hot and humid). This is also a good opportunity to have a buddy check to make sure that everyone is present and that no one has wandered off.

- Keep your group visible. When traveling in any format (on foot, bike, or canoe) always make sure that you can see the entire group or, depending on the terrain, that you can see the person in front and the person in back of you. Make sure that all participants understand that they need to keep the people behind them and the people in front of them in clear view.

- The group should go only as fast as the slowest participant. Not everyone is going to travel at the same speed. Even though it might take longer, this is a good way to keep everyone together.

- Everyone should carry a whistle to use only as a signal for help should trouble arise. Remember that whistles are for emergency use only.

- Participants should listen carefully, particularly when you are going over where to travel and any other safety concerns you as the leader might have. Make sure that everyone in the group understands what needs to happen, what is allowed, and what is not allowed.

- The leader, especially, should know how to recognize any poisonous plants or snakes in the area.

- Everyone should avoid strangers.

- Participants should tell the leader about suspicious sounds, activities, or people in the area.

- Everyone should know to stay on the trail or road and move toward familiar people and/or lights if they are in trouble.

- Participants should know where to go in case of illness or injury, whether that's to the leader, base site, camp infirmary, the school nurse, or to the phone to dial 911.

Health and Safety Agreements

Develop an individual or group health and safety agreement. This involves brainstorming with your group a list of health and safety practices while on site or on trail. Have each individual contribute to the list and sign it as an agreement to observe the rules. This is an opportunity to discuss the rules as well as clarify why they are in place. Doing so is an additional step toward understanding the rules for participants as well as a means for each person to accept responsibility for the health, safety, and well being of the entire group.

Safety is the primary concern on any trip. Be sure to go over these rules and ask participants if there are any other rules that will need to be followed. Certain activities will have specific rules. For example, if you are traveling by canoe, be sure that all participants understand that they need to wear their lifejackets at all times and that they are not to stand up in a canoe at any time. Following simple safety rules will help everyone have the best experience possible.

Weather

Red sky at night, sailors' delight. Red sky in morning, sailors take warning. This popular weather saying reminded sailors and pioneers that if the sky was red at sunset, they would have fair sailing in the morning, but if the sky was red in the morning, they needed to prepare for wet and sometimes stormy weather. Before the days of sophisticated weather instruments, pioneers, explorers, sailors, and trappers predicted weather by what the sky and clouds looked like to help them prepare for their journeys.

Although some may still follow the advice of this saying today, people who are planning any outdoor activity still rely on more sophisticated weather reports so that rain, snow, excessive heat or cold, or high wind won't surprise them. Weather changes can be uncomfortable or even dangerous. Unlike the preinformation era, most people can get the weather information they need from the local newspaper or from television. If, however, you're on a trip of two or more days, you must rely on your own ability to understand potential weather changes.

Helpful Hint

If you are in a national, state, or county park, check in with the local ranger for the local forecast.

Weather means daily changes in temperature, humidity, wind, cloud cover, and precipitation. Throughout the world, most weather comes from the west and moves east. In mountainous areas, however, you may encounter storms caused by changes in air temperature as the elevation increases. These weather changes may be quite different from those in the valley from which you came.

To understand the weather — and, in particular, rain or snow — you need to understand the water cycle and the way in which clouds form.

Water moves in a cycle. When the sun heats the earth, it also heats lakes, streams, rivers, and oceans where the water is evaporated or transpired through plants and trees, and rises into the sky on warm air. As warm air rises from the ground, laden with the moisture from these rivers, streams, oceans, and plants, it cools, creating clouds or condensation. As the clouds rise higher, the air becomes colder. When clouds become so cold that they can no longer hold moisture, the moisture falls back to earth in the form of rain or snow (precipitation), and the process starts all over again. See chapter 5, "Exploring Your World," for more detailed information on the water cycle.

Most weather systems in the United States come from the Pacific Ocean and move east in convection currents. When air moves east and meets the Cascades, the Sierras, and the Rocky Mountains, it must rise to get over the mountains. As it rises, the air cools, and clouds form. If the clouds are heavy with moisture and the air cool to the point of condensation, rain or snow falls. After the air crosses one of these mountain ranges, it keeps going east, and because the air has already dropped much of its moisture, the eastern side of the mountain range is relatively dry compared with the western side. As the air passes over the prairie states, it picks up new moisture rising from fields, lakes, rivers, and forests; rain falls again when the air is sufficiently cool and saturated.

Weather is an important factor in learning outdoor living skills. Preparing for weather and planning the appropriate equipment and materials is essential to having a positive experience. Understanding the sun, temperature, humidity, clouds, wind, and severe weather are all important if you are to have a safe and successful outdoor program.

Sun

We all like to work outside especially when it's sunny; however, you need to be aware of the sun and the exposure your group has to it. Have guidelines for all participants in your group to follow when outside with long exposure to the sun. The most common effect of sun exposure is sunburn. Simple preventative measures can be made to help reduce the amount of exposure to the sun and the harmful ultraviolet rays associated with it. Wearing a broad-brimmed hat, wrap-around sunglasses, and quality clothing with long sleeves and a collar and applying sunscreen to areas of exposed skin regularly throughout the day will all help reduce the risk of sun exposure. Have additional items of protective clothing and sunscreen on hand for those group members who may have forgotten to bring them. Research recommends that sunscreen should have an SPF (Sun Protection Factor) of at least 15 and be a "broad spectrum type." Sunscreen should also be waterproof if possible so that it doesn't wear off when participants sweat.

Helpful Hint

The SPF factor is based on the length one can stay in the sun. For example, an SPF factor of 15 means it would take 15 times longer to sunburn than if you didn't use sunscreen at all.

Temperature

Temperature is a key factor in planning your OLS outing. You will plan what to bring in regard to clothing and sleeping material based partially on the temperature.

In mountainous areas such as the Rockies or the Smokeys in the United States, temperatures can be warm during the day and much cooler at night. Likewise, in the desert or arid regions the temperatures can be over 100°F during the day and almost freezing (32°F) at night. Be prepared for all kinds of weather even if the forecast doesn't call for it (forecasters have been known to be wrong at times).

Because weather, and especially temperature, can be unpredictable, expect the unexpected. It's pretty rare that temperatures will go from very cold to very hot in a matter of minutes, but the temperature can drop from a warm temperature (shorts and a t-shirt) to a very cold temperature (hats, gloves, and a jacket) rapidly. This is especially true in higher altitudes or the northern climates of the United States or other mountainous regions of the world.

Humidity

The amount of water vapor in the air is called humidity. Air is like a sponge. Sometimes, a sponge has no moisture; at other times, it's damp, very wet, or so saturated that it can't hold any more moisture. Relative humidity is the amount of moisture in the air compared with the maximum amount that the air can hold. "Relative humidity of 65 percent" means that the air contains 65 percent of the moisture that it can hold at the current temperature. Humidity combined with the temperature will indicate how comfortable or uncomfortable the weather may be, given the amount of moisture in the air. When humidity reaches 100 percent, the clouds can hold no more moisture, and the excess moisture falls as rain or snow.

Understanding relative humidity, therefore, can help you decide what to wear and the amount of exercise to do, as well as how much drinking water to take along. The more humid and hot it is, the more water your body will lose. Therefore, you should bring along extra water and stop frequently to drink. Also on hot and humid days your body loses not just water but also salt through the sweating process. Be sure to have snacks and foods with a high salt content or sports drinks available to help replace the lost salt.

ACA File Photo

Clouds

Clouds are important to understand in that clouds indicate a chance of precipitation. All clouds have some sort of moisture associated with them. Knowing what types of clouds are in the area may help you determine if you will encounter precipitation. Clouds that are formed by rising air currents are classified as cumulus clouds, because they are piled up, or are "accumulated formations." Stratus clouds are formed without any vertical movement such as fog and are sheet-like in nature. Clouds can be classified as being high, middle, or low.

High clouds form in the cold upper part of the atmosphere, are made up of tiny ice crystals, and can include cirrus clouds, cirrocumulus clouds, and cirrostratus clouds. Cirrus clouds are thin, wispy, feathery clouds forming above 25,000 feet; they're often called "mares' tails" because they resemble the tails of horses streaming in the wind. Cirrocumulus clouds, which form between 20,000 and 25,000 feet, are rippled and thin. Many years ago, fishermen called these clouds "mackerel scales" because they looked like the scales of the mackerel the men caught off the coasts of New England and Canada. Cirrostratus clouds, which are sheets of high ice clouds, are responsible for the halo you sometimes see around the sun or moon. Light shines only so far through the thin layer of clouds, producing the halo effect.

Middle clouds form about 10,000 feet above the earth and are classified as either altostratus or altocumulus. Altostratus clouds are veils or sheet clouds, sometimes with stripes. Altocumulus clouds are patches or layers of puffy clouds.

Low clouds are usually sheet-like or stratus formations, can produce drizzle, are dull gray, and resemble fog. They form anywhere from just above the earth to about 10,000 feet and include nimbostratus clouds and stratocumulus clouds. Nimbostratus clouds are rain sheets. Stratocumulus clouds are irregular masses of clouds in rolling or puffy layers. Stratocumulus clouds don't produce rain, but they can change into nimbostratus clouds, which are rain producers. (Figure 4.1)

Figure 4.1

Other cloud types can include cumulonimbus clouds or cumulus clouds. Cumulonimbus clouds are also known as common thunderheads. Their bases may be almost on the ground, and their heads may rise to 75,000 feet. The top of a growing thunderhead often looks like a head of cauliflower. Generally where there is a cumulonimbus cloud, there is a good chance of rain and severe weather. Cumulus clouds are puffy clouds with changing shapes. Cumulus clouds are often called "fair-weather clouds," because they form during the day, rise, and disappear at night.

Wind

Wind occurs because of horizontal and vertical pressure differences in the earth's atmosphere. Wind can add to or take away from the comfort level in the out-of-doors. In cooler weather, wind can make the air feel like it is actually colder than the temperature says. This is known as the wind chill factor. Meteorologists determine the wind chill by factoring the actual temperature and the velocity of the wind to determine the cooling power of wind on bare skin. Wind chill can be critical in extremely cold temperatures where frostbite can occur more rapidly than if the wind were not blowing. In warmer weather, wind can be a welcome relief in the heat of the day. Wind can also turn a moderate snowfall into a blinding blizzard or kick up a duststorm in the desert. Be aware of the potential for wind and how that may affect your outdoor activity so that you can plan for the unexpected.

The direction of the wind can also affect your trip. Winds that come out of the north in the northern hemisphere tend to be colder than winds that come out of the south. Likewise, winds that come out of the south in the southern hemisphere tend to be cooler than winds that come out of the north because of the location of the equator and the polar ice caps.

Teachable Moment: Making a Wind Direction Finder

A wind direction finder will help you identify which direction the wind is coming from. (Figure 4.2)

Materials Needed: metal coat hanger, tin can lid from a No. 10 tin can, an eyedropper without a bulb, masking tape, nail, wooden dowel, four pegs

Tools Needed: metal or wire cutter, gloves to protect your hands, hammer, compass

Follow these instructions:

- Cut an arrowhead and counterweight out of the tin-can lid and use masking tape to tape the edges to prevent someone from getting cut.

- Bend the coat hanger so that it's straight and cut off the badly bent ends.

- Bend an oval loop in each end of the straightened coat hanger.

- Use the masking tape to stick the arrowhead against one loop and the counterweight against the loop on the other end.

- Find the balance point on the straightened coat hanger by resting it on one finger to see at what point it will balance.

- Bend a loop, the diameter of your eyedropper at the balance point and insert the eyedropper into the loop.

- Drive a nail into the top of a dowel and clip the head off the nail.

- Set the eyedropper down over the nail.

- Stick the dowel of your wind direction finder in the ground.

- Locate north with a compass, and place a peg in the ground on the north side of the wind direction finder. You can also place a peg for east, south, and west.

- When the wind blows, the arrow should always point to the direction the wind is blowing. Remember that wind direction is always stated by where the wind is coming from.

Severe Weather

The combination of the sun, temperature, humidity, clouds, and wind can lead to severe weather. Severe weather can include rain, thunderstorms, hail, and tornadoes. Know the potential for severe weather in the area where you will be and use the following precautions.

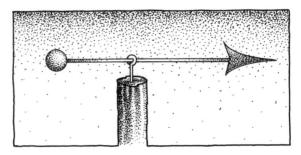

Figure 4.2

Rain

It is possible to participate in an outdoor activity in the rain as long as the group is prepared and has the appropriate clothing and, most important, it's safe to do so. If conditions become unsafe (such as slippery footing or lightning appearing in the area), stop and seek shelter until the weather improves. When the conditions are such that it is okay to continue, keep the following safety factors in mind.

Safety Tips

- Rain coats, rain pants, and other bulky clothing may impede motion.

- Visibility may be restricted, especially for people wearing glasses.

- Footing can turn precarious as the ground becomes slippery.

- Being in the rain for a long period of time may lead to hypothermia as participants get wet or the temperature drops.

Thunderstorms

Thunderstorms generally follow a buildup of thunderhead clouds, and where there is thunder, there is lightning. Knowing how to identify when it is likely to storm will help you find suitable protection or shelter when out in remote areas.

Keep your eye on the sky. Whenever you see thunderhead clouds building up or hear thunder in the distance, prepare to take cover. Use the following procedures if caught in a thunderstorm.

Safety Tips

- Attempt to get to a building or a car wherever possible. If this is not a possibility, get to an open space and squat on the ground as low as possible.

- If you are in a wooded area, find a location protected by a low clump of trees. NEVER stand under a single large tree in the open.

- Avoid tall structures such as towers, tall trees, fences, telephone lines, or power lines.

- Stay away from natural lightning rods such as golf clubs, tractors, fishing rods, bicycles, camping equipment, or any metal objects.

- Stay away from rivers, lakes, or other bodies of water.

- If you are isolated in a level field or prairie and you feel your hair stand on end (which indicates that lightning is about to strike), bend forward, putting your hands on your knees. A position with feet together and crouching while removing all metal objects is recommended. Do not lie flat on the ground.

- If you're on a lake, go to the nearest shore at once and take cover.

- The best practice during a thunderstorm is to get away from high places and bodies of water and to seek shelter under small trees until you're sure that the storm has passed. There may be lingering lightning strikes, so don't rush right out into the rain; wait at least 20 minutes. Storms can come up suddenly, and with storms come the possibility of rain, hail, and tornadoes.

Hail

Hail is produced by many strong thunderstorms. Not only can hail be smaller than a pea or as large as a softball, but it can also be very destructive to plants and a danger to those caught out in a storm. In a hailstorm, the size of hailstones can change suddenly. It is important to take cover immediately!

Tornadoes

The most violent of atmospheric storms is a tornado, often referred to as a "twister." Even though tornadoes can occur in almost any state at any time given the right conditions, spring is traditionally the most active time. Tornadoes can be the most dangerous and terrifying of weather conditions because the wind has been clocked at up to 300 miles per hour and destroys anything in its path, which can range in width from inches to up to a mile.

Signs of an approaching tornado include:

- changes in the sky (it may have a blackish green tint),

- wind may die down to a standstill, and

- a cloud of debris.

It is recommended, when possible, to have a portable radio with your group to listen to the most current and updated forecasts. When a tornado watch (an alert by the National Weather Service stating that the conditions are right for tornadoes to occur) is issued, review with your group the procedures in place for what to do in the event of a tornado. If the weather is going to be severe, you may want to err on the side of caution and take shelter until the storms pass. When a tornado warning (an alert by the National Weather Service stating that a tornado has been sighted or indicated by weather radar) occurs, take cover immediately! If you do not have access to a radio or any other means of communication and you suspect the conditions are right for a tornado, take cover immediately!

Safety Tips

- If possible, get inside a building.

- Go to the basement, storm cellar, or the lowest level of the building.

- If there is no basement, go to an inner hallway or a smaller inner room without windows, such as a bathroom or closet.

- Get away from the windows. Most injuries are caused by flying glass and debris.

- Go to the center of the room. Stay away from corners because they tend to attract debris.

- Get under a piece of sturdy furniture such as a workbench or heavy table or desk and hold on to it.

- Use arms to protect head and neck.

- If shelter is not available or there is no time to get indoors, lie in a ditch or low-lying area or crouch near a strong building.

For more information on severe weather visit the Federal Emergency Management Agency at www.fema.com.

Drinking Water

At home, it's easy to find good drinking water; all you have to do is turn on the faucet. Outdoors, it's not quite as simple. If you're at a youth camp or a state, national, or city park that has faucets, you can expect good drinking water. Health regulations in the United States mandate that water pumped through pipes from which the general public will drink must contain no disease-bearing organisms such as coloform bacteria or E. coli. Organizations or agencies that provide water to the public must perform an annual water test on all wells usable by the public. In all other cases, you must treat or purify the water.

Until about the 1970s, most canoeists, backpackers, mountain climbers, and rafters simply drank from rivers and streams, giving little thought to any impurities in the water. Today, outdoor enthusiasts need to take precautions against disease-causing organisms in even the most remote streams.

ACA File Photo

A good example of a water-borne organism is Giardia lamblia, which causes a disease called giardiasis. This disease, which has been around for many years, is now found even in the most remote high mountain areas; the organism seems to thrive in the cold waters of mountain streams. No one knows how Giardia came to the United States or where it evolved. The organism is spread to water sources by human and animal fecal material, and anyone who drinks Giardia-contaminated water suffers a very painful complication of the intestinal tract; Giardia acts as a powerful laxative. The illness may take up to two weeks to show up, and victims may be ill for many months.

The solution to this dilemma is water purification. You must purify all water that you'll be using for drinking, cooking, and washing dishes. To purify water, you first need to select a source and then purify it using a variety of methods including water filtration, water purifiers, boiling, and chemical treatment.

Selecting a Water Source

If public or treated water is not available and you must purify the water you use, practice it at your base camp before venturing forth on your trip to learn how the method works and how long it takes. Then when you get to a water source on the trip, you'll be able to act with confidence and assurance that you know what to do.

Select a source where the water is relatively clean and free from agricultural or chemical wastes. If possible, choose a source that is still and clear, as many microorganisms tend to remain suspended in water that is turbulent (such as running stream water). Avoid using water sources where animal activity or human impact is obvious and avoid streams carrying runoff from farms, forestry operations, and factories.

When you're hiking in a cold or snowy area, find clean white snow or ice. Ice is preferred because it has a greater water content; however, keep in mind that many bacteria are resistant to the cold and will still be in the water when melted. If the snow has a pinkish tint to it, beware that this may be contaminated with a toxic algae that will not be filtered out through the purifying process. When you melt snow for drinking water, pack it tightly before you put it in a pan over the heat source. By doing so, you'll use less fuel and end up with more drinking water.

Water sources vary in different geographical areas. Talk with forest rangers, expert campers, and experienced outdoor leaders in the area where you'll be traveling; they can give you the best advice.

Mechanical Treatment

Mechanical treatment can include filtration or purification. Both methods force water through a finely porous mesh that is housed in a filtration unit. Both the filter and the purifier are microbiological water treatment devices. The difference between the two units is that the filter removes protozoa and bacteria from contaminated water and the purifier takes it one step further and eliminates viruses (such as hepatitis A). The process is safer and more convenient than it used to be and has emerged as the most popular method for water treatment. Filters and purifiers are small units that require hand pumping to filter the water through the meshing. They come in a variety of sizes and styles and vary as to what type of organisms they eliminate.

When shopping for a filter or purifier, find out the size and weight, the type of elements it removes (for example, bacteria, protozoa, Giardia, or E. coli), if it's cleanable in the field, and how much it pumps. The type of filter cartridge is also important. Cartridges are made from either fiberglass or ceramic. Both are effective in straining out pathogens; however, the ceramic cartridge is easier to clean and lasts longer. The fiberglass cartridge doesn't last as long and will need to be replaced when it clogs. If you are traveling in an area where the water is apt to have more elements in it (such as turbid water) or traveling with a group, a ceramic filter will work best. It is important to know all of these things depending on where you are going, the size of the group, and how much equipment you want to carry. Prices for filters and purifiers can range from $35 to $250.

Remember that mechanical cartridges will clog (it shows that they are working), so they must be replaced or cleaned at intervals to keep them efficient. Be sure to follow the directions that come with your group's water filter and have additional filters on hand to replace any that might clog or you can't clean. Keep directions in a readily available file at home and make a copy for your trip so that you can refer to them when needed.

Boiling Water

Boiling water is another way to purify water, is a simple task, and is considered 100 percent effective against almost all microorganisms and viruses. Simply bring water to a rolling boil for ten minutes; however, at higher elevations (over 3000 feet), boiling time should be extended an additional three minutes. There are a few disadvantages to boiling: it takes time, drains your fuel supply, and will not remove the sediment from the water, so it could taste gritty. Also remember to sanitize your water bottle by rinsing it out with some of the boiling water before adding clean water to it.

Chemical Treatment

If you use a chemical treatment, otherwise known as halogens, such as iodine or a bromine or chlorine compound, you should be able to kill most bacteria and viruses. However, hard-shelled protozoan cysts, such as cryptosporidia are strongly resistant to iodine and chlorine and may not be killed. The best defense against these bacteria, viruses, and protozoans is to combine chemical filtration with chemical treatment for maximum effectiveness.

It is extremely important to follow the directions when using iodine or chlorine to make sure that you are adding enough, but not too much, to the water. There are a few drawbacks to using halogens. Water treated with iodine can have a taste that many people do not like and iodine can be unhealthy to some people, including women who are pregnant and people with a thyroid condition who use it for longer than 14 days.

Add tablets to the water and wait 10 to 15 minutes for them to dissolve before using. For cold water, the wait time should be between 30 and 60 minutes. Do not use, add to, or drink water until after the wait period.

Chlorine is also effective against bacteria and viruses in purifying water. Add eight drops of liquid chlorine bleach to one gallon of water. Be sure that the bleach has no other active ingredient other than 4 to 6 percent sodium hypochlorite (check the product's ingredients label).

Disposal of Human Waste

One of the biggest challenges of using the outdoors for recreation is disposing of human waste. Human waste carries many forms of bacteria that are harmful to the environment and to humans, and it's just plain disagreeable to people who encounter it by accident. Urine, however, doesn't cause bacterial problems; it's a sterile waste product that usually carries no parasites. It does, however, contain uric acid, which, when crystallized, has a taste that bears, skunks, and particularly porcupines enjoy. Urine also has a disagreeable odor, particularly when it gets on clothing or accumulates in one place. When living in the out-of-doors, you will eventually need to establish a facility for waste disposal.

Established toilet facilities or latrines should be used if they are available. If established sites are not available, then the preferred method is a cathole. A cathole is a small hole at least 6 inches deep, and it should be at least 200 feet from any water source, campsite, or trail. The cathole is dug, used once, and then covered and packed down tight. Do not put anything other than human waste in the cathole. Paper products such as toilet paper or feminine hygiene products should be packed out in a separate bag and thrown out in the garbage on your return from the woods.

Although they are strongly discouraged for general use, latrines may be appropriate with larger groups (ten or more) or younger children that are staying at a site for an extended period of time. Dig a long trench 12 inches deep, and ask users to start at one end and cover their waste as they use the facility. When the trench is full to within 4 inches of the surface, cover it and start another one.

Any area that you dig, whether it is a cathole or latrine, should be covered up well enough to look like no one was there. Leave the area as it was. Do not place stones, rocks, or other matter over the area to cover it up.

Blue Ridge Camp, Georgia

Relieving yourself on river trips has some specific protocals. Each river has a different management plan. Check with the U.S. Forest Service, the National Park Service, or the Bureau of Land Management (if the river you plan to travel is managed by one of these federal agencies) to find out how you should dispose of human waste. Where there are no established rules and regulations, take the following steps:

- Urinate and defecate above the high water mark and at least 200 feet away from the river. Keep away from natural drainage systems.

- Dig a cathole at least 200 feet away from a water source, trail, or campsite.

- Carry out all toilet paper or feminine hygiene products in plastic bags.

Some wilderness areas may require you to pack out all solid human waste. Check with the local resource managers for any recommendations they might have. Making a rocket-box porta-potty for large groups staying in an area for a longer duration may be of assistance. You'll also need a toilet seat, large heavy-duty plastic bags, a chemical deodorant (such as the kind used in motor homes) or chlorine bleach to prevent methane gas production, toilet paper, and a bucket for hand washing.

Teachable Moment: Building and Using a Rocket-Box

Materials Needed: ammo or other sealable box, heavy-duty plastic bags, chemical deodorant or chlorine bleach, toilet paper, bucket or hand sanitizer

Follow these instructions:

- Line the box with two plastic bags, folding the excess plastic over the edges.

- Pour in the deodorant.

- Use the toilet for fecal material, not for urine. Urine will increase the amount of liquids that you must transport from your campsite.

- Place used toilet paper, tampons, and sanitary napkins in the toilet.

- Keep the hand washing bucket nearby (covered with plastic, if flies are a problem). Hand sanitizer or individual antiseptic packets can work as well.

- To dismantle the toilet for the next day's trip, remove the plastic bags from the ammo box, squeeze out excess air, and tie the tops of the bags shut.

- Place the used bags inside other bags, and store them in the ammo box for transportation in one of the canoes or rafts. As other bags are used, add them to the carrying bags.

- At the next stop, remove the bag containing the used bags from the ammo box and line the box with two new plastic bags.

- When the trip is over, dispose of the plastic bags in a proper disposal area.

Deciding the most efficient and practical way to dispose of human waste properly requires planning and know-how. Before hitting the trail, check with the local resource manager as to the best recommendation for the area you will be visiting.

First Aid

First aid is immediate and temporary care given to the victim of an accident or sudden illness. The person or people with the appropriate certifications in first aid should render assistance to anyone who is ill or injured. It is not the purpose of this book to give the reader a complete first aid course. There are many excellent courses on first aid and wilderness first aid. Someone

ACA File Photo

in your organization should have an appropriate and current certification in first aid and cardiopulmonary resuscitation (CPR). Use the following as a guideline:

- When access to the emergency medical system (EMS) is 20 minutes or less, certification by a nationally recognized provider of training in first aid and CPR is needed.

- When access to EMS is 20 to 60 minutes, certification by a nationally recognized provider of training in second-level first aid and CPR (for example, Responding to Emergencies or Emergency Response, Advanced First Aid or First Responder) is needed.

- When access to emergency rescue systems or EMS is more than one hour away, certification from a nationally recognized provider of training in wilderness first aid and CPR is needed.

The following section provides basic information about common problems that may occur when participating in an outdoor program.

Cold and Hypothermia

Cold weather can set in at the drop of a hat. If you are planning on being in the outdoors, you should be prepared for the cold with layers, layers, layers! One way to prepare for the cold besides having warm clothing along is to layer the clothing you are wearing. Wearing a long-sleeved shirt, a sweatshirt, a vest, a jacket, and a hat allows you to remove layers if you are too warm and to replace them when you start getting colder. Despite all this prevention, even the best layers or cold weather prevention will not always keep out the cold.

Not only does the cold make you tire faster, but it can also lead to hypothermia. Hypothermia is a life-threatening condition that occurs when the body cannot produce heat as fast as it is being lost so that the body's temperature falls below 95°F. It can happen outdoors, indoors, in southern states, and even on a summer day. Signs of hypothermia can include shivering, disorientation or change in mental status, loss of consciousness, and potentially death.

Should members of your group show signs of hypothermia, treat the condition immediately. Get them to a warm building, shelter, or tent. If no shelter is immediately available, a warm fire or blankets or sleeping bags will also help get them warm. If they are in wet clothing, have them remove it and put on dry clothing. For mild cases of hypothermia (core temperature

90°F and above), give them hot liquids to drink or an energy bar to help increase their core temperature. For more severe cases of hypothermia (core temperature is below 90°F) call EMS or get them to medical attention as soon as possible. Move the patient as little as possible. For more information about hypothermia and how to treat it, refer to a national organization for first aid or someone with current certification in first aid training or higher.

If the weather does not improve or members of your group are beginning to get cold, you may want to end the activity for the day or take a break until participants have warmed up.

Heat and Heat-Related Illnesses

Just as the weather can get cold, it can also get warm or even hot. Warm weather can be a pleasure to work in, but we again need to be prepared for hot weather that might affect conditions during the program.

It is incredibly important, especially in hot and humid weather, that all participants drink plenty of water or sports drinks. Juice and soda are not always wise choices because they contain sugar, which can dehydrate the body. Make sure that all participants have access to plenty of fresh water and are taking time out to drink it. To ensure this, stop intermittently for a water break and also make sure that they are drinking it with their meals before they drink anything else. A good rule of thumb is to drink one cup (8 oz.) of water every 20 minutes when recreating. It is also better to drink in small sips versus large gulps. Wipe cool water on exposed areas of the skin or even periodically dip clothing in water to help cool the body on warm or hot days. A wet bandana tied around the neck is sometimes helpful as long as it is not a safety hazard.

Recreating in warm or hot conditions can lead to heat emergencies. Heat cramps (sudden painful muscular spasms), heat exhaustion (heavy perspiration characterized by normal or slightly above normal body temperatures), or heat stroke (hot, dry skin, no sweating, unresponsiveness, or altered mental status) are all serious heat-related emergencies that can occur, with heat stroke being the most severe. Participants should be appropriately dressed for the weather, take plenty of breaks to have water and rest in the shade, and stop when they are tired. If a heat emergency arises, it is important to cool the body down as rapidly as possible and stop cooling as soon as the mental status improves. Continuing to cool when the body temperature has returned to normal can lead to hypothermia. For more information about treating heat-related illnesses, refer to a national organization for first aid or someone with current certification in first aid training or higher.

Depending on the activity, you may need to adjust your plan. If the activity you are doing requires participants to be in long pants and sleeves (walking through a brushy area), you may want to have them do this early in the morning or late in the afternoon when it's cooler. The warmest temperature of the day is usually between 11 A.M. and 3 P.M. If it is really hot and humid, you may want to rest during these hours for the safety of the group.

Chapped Hands and Lips

Chapped hands and lips can be caused by exposure to the wind or sun. Protect the chapped parts of the body from further exposure to the elements. Apply lotion to hands or a commercial lip balm to help reduce the dryness. Many lip balms and lotions also come with an SPF factor for protection against the ultraviolet rays the sun produces. For chapping that is more extreme, follow proper procedure from a nationally recognized provider of training for first aid.

Dehydration

Dehydration can happen on hot or cold days when the body does not get enough water or other fluids. Be sure that your group has an ample supply of water and make sure that they are drinking water throughout the activity. Signs and symptoms of dehydration can include

• Headache caused by excessive loss of fluid from vomiting, urinating, or sweating

• Dry mouth where the participant is thirsty or doesn't drink at all

To care for victims of dehydration follow the proper procedure for first aid from a nationally recognized provider.

Common Headaches

Headaches can happen due to injury, illness, or dehydration. Follow the proper procedure from a nationally recognized provider of first aid. Do not administer any medications unless under written instruction from a physician affiliated with your organization.

Insect Bites and Stings

Insect bites and stings can be an annoyance to some people and cause severe allergic reactions in others. Participants who are already aware of their allergy to bee or wasp stings should have their own medication (generally an Epi-Pen) and usually know how to administer it. To treat any insect sting or severe reactions, follow the proper procedure in first aid from a nationally recognized provider.

Muscle Cramps

Muscle cramps can happen when the muscles are not properly warmed up or not properly stretched or when the participant is dehydrated. Be sure that all participants stretch and warm up properly before starting out on your journey and also any time after a rest stop. Make sure that everyone is also drinking plenty of water. To treat muscle cramps, follow the proper procedure from a nationally recognized provider of first aid.

For all additional illnesses and injuries that can occur, consult with a nationally recognized provider of fist aid for proper care and treatment.

First Aid Kit

Carry a fully stocked first aid kit that is big enough to treat minor medical emergencies and control major medical emergencies. Your first aid kit should be well stocked for the number of people in your group as well as the duration of your trip. Anytime you or someone in your group performs any type of first aid, be sure to follow universal precautions such as wearing gloves when you are treating someone. Complete information about universal precautions can be accessed from a nationally recognized provider of first aid. Prestocked kits can be purchased through a variety of vendors to supply as few as 2 people or as many as 100, depending on the size of the kit. Wherever you get your first aid kit, use the following as a guideline for the supplies you will need. Make sure that the first aid kit is with you and the group at all times. To leave it in the van or at your campsite while on a half-day hike renders it useless. First aid kits should be in a waterproof container and include the following:

Group Size: 25	
Item	**Quantity**
Plastic Adhesive Bandages – 1" x 3"	16
Woven Adhesive Bandages – 1" x 3"	16
Woven Adhesive Bandages – Med Fingertip	10
Woven Adhesive Bandages – Knuckle	8
Bandage Compress – 2"	4
Bandage Compress – 4"	1
Burn Cream – 1/8 oz.	6
Burn Dressing Unit – Burn Gel/2 Pads/Tape	1
CPR Mask	1
Cold Pack – 5" x 7"	1
Eye Dressing Unit – Eyewash/2 Pads/Tape	1
Gauze Compress – 24" x 72"	1
Latex Gloves (pairs)	4
Insect Sting Swabs	10
Iodine Wipes	10
Triangular Bandage w/Pins – 40" x 40"	1
Triple-Antibiotic Ointment – 1 gram	10
Wire Splint	1
Towelettes	10
Tourniquet	1
Tweezers	1
Major Trauma Dressing	1
Splinter Remover	1
Scissors	1

You should also have:

- medical forms (including a release for permission to treat statement) for all participants in the group;

- flashlight;

- paper and pencil to write down any accidents, injuries, or treatments that might occur; and

- sunscreen with an SPF of 15 or higher.

Some participants may be allergic or sensitive to sunscreen and may have their own. Be sure to ask participants if they have used sunscreen before or have had reactions to sunscreen before allowing them to apply it.

Plants and Animals

The environment is full of many wonderful, interesting, and exciting things to observe. Literally thousands of animals, plants, and insects coexist together in various environments from the rainforests of the Amazon to the tundra of Siberia to your own backyard. Although it is fun to explore various parts of the ecosystem and its inhabitants, you and your group need to keep several things in mind.

Animals

Although many animals that you will encounter on your outings are cute, fuzzy, and cuddly looking, they are still wild. The best way to view animals is at a distance. Don't encourage animals to come closer by enticing them with food, just to get a better look at them. This creates a situation where the animal will associate humans with food and may create a serious hazard that could put you and your group at risk. Many animals such as raccoons carry diseases such as rabies, which also pose a threat. Animals do not intentionally harm humans. When humans are injured by an animal, chances are other factors (such as coming between a mother bear and her cub) contributed to the incident. Keep in mind that when animals see you in their habitat, it is just as unusual for them as it would be for you to see a stranger in your home. Be considerate, give them plenty of room, and use caution; any animal can be unpredictable.

Traveling in Bear Country

Many areas of the United States are home to bears. The United States has a variety of species including the black bear (*Ursus americanas*) and the brown bear (*Ursus arctos*) or grizzly bear, with black bears being more common throughout the country. Bears are typically seen in national parks such as Yellowstone, Glacier, Olympic, and Yosemite, but they can also be found in other parts of the country including county and state parks and national forests. Does that mean that you can't go on your outing because bears are in the area? Absolutely not, but you need to keep in mind a few tips to maintain safety when traveling in bear country.

The Bear Facts

Bears are fast animals. Although they certainly don't look it, a bear can run over 30 miles per hour, faster than any Olympic sprinter. Bears have poorly developed eyesight but smell and hear very well. All black bears, grizzly cubs, and some adult grizzlies can climb trees. A typical male black bear can weigh

300 pounds, while the female weighs about 230 pounds. A typical male grizzly bear weighs on average about 550 pounds, although they can weigh as much as 1100 pounds. Female grizzlies weigh about half of their adult male counterparts. Bears that stand up on their hind legs are not threatening you but are just trying to identify you.

Safety Tips

- Be alert at all times.

- Make as much noise as possible when walking down trails. Sing or shout to warn bears of your presence.

- Never intentionally approach a bear.

- Do not hike after dark.

- If you encounter a bear, DO NOT RUN! If the bear is unaware of your presence, detour quietly and rapidly away. Give the bear plenty of room.

- If you spot a bear, try to stay upwind of the animal.

- BACK AWAY SLOWLY if the bear is aware of you, waving your arms over your head (it makes you appear bigger) and talking in a low, calming voice.

- Do not corner a bear or any other animal. Allow them plenty of space and an escape route.

- If a bear makes contact with you, play dead. Lie face down, curl up with your knees against your chest and your arms and hands laced around your neck, and don't move. Leave your pack on your back for protection.

- Treat all adult bears as if there are cubs nearby. Never get between a mother and her cub.

- Be alert to signs (such as droppings, diggings, and tracks), sounds, or other indications of bears.

- Use one of the three options in chapter 6, "Putting It on Your Plate," to protect your food when in base camp.

- Take photos at a distance or with a telephoto lens.

- Remember that although bears are cute and cuddly looking, they are still wild animals and can be dangerous if provoked or intimidated. Never underestimate the power of a bear or its instinct to protect itself, its young, and its territory.

Poisonous Critters

Snakes may or may not be poisonous. Some poisonous snakes such as a rattlesnake are easily identifiable; however, others may not be. Be familiar with the location you are going to and the poisonous snakes that may be in the area.

Various species of marine life can also pose a problem to human visitors. Obvious predators of the sea are the wide variety of sharks that may swim in shallow waters of the ocean when feeding on schools of fish. Other species such as jellyfish or the Portuguese man-of-war have stingers in their tentacles, which help them capture food. Although usually feared by ocean swimmers, jellyfish are for the most part harmless. However, curious observers or unknowing swimmers or waders can receive painful stings, which can result in a mild rash or even death in severe cases.

Many insects can also bite or sting. Insects such as scorpions, bees, or wasps sting and inflict painful injections, which can lead to tenderness and swelling in the sting area. People who have severe reactions to such stings usually carry an Epi-Pen, which can help reduce the severity of the reaction.

The black widow spider is the most venomous spider in North America. This spider is easily recognizable by its black body and the red hourglass on its abdomen. Anyone who is bitten by a black widow needs immediate medical attention. Its close cousin, the brown recluse, also produces a venomous bite, but it is not as serious as that of the black widow. Its trademark fiddle shape on the topside of its body identifies the brown recluse. Because many of these insects like dark places, participants should check their shoes before putting them on and look before reaching into a dark place.

Plants

Some plants can also produce allergic reactions. The most well-known poisonous plants are poison ivy, poison oak, and poison sumac. Signs and symptoms usually occur within 12 to 48 hours and include severe itching, redness of the skin, and blistering. If your group has been in an area with poisonous plants, participants should immediately rinse exposed areas with cold water. Washing with soap and water may be helpful within the first 30 minutes from the point of contact. Poison ivy can also be contracted from handling clothes or pets that have been in contact with the poisonous plants or even burning wood with poison ivy vines still attached. To treat poison ivy, poison oak, or poison sumac, follow proper procedure by a nationally recognized provider of first aid.

Stinging nettles, which are covered with small, invisible stinging hairs, produce an intense pain when brushed against. Although the reaction may be seen in small, white, itchy bumps after contact and is certainly annoying, the reaction is relatively harmless and goes away after a short time. It is helpful to teach your group to recognize the poisonous plants in the area that you will be in.

Safety Tip

If anyone in your group is bitten or stung by an animal or insect or has a reaction that cannot be explained, follow proper procedure from a nationally recognized provider of first aid to treat the problem or seek medical attention.

Summary

Wherever you decide to travel and practice outdoor living skills, it is important to keep weather, water, waste disposal, first aid, and animals, insects, and plants in mind to ensure a safe trip. Prior planning and proper minimal impact practices will ensure that the group has the best outing possible and that the environment is minimally impacted. Checking in with the city, county, state, or national forest and parks personnel will ensure you have the most updated information in regard to weather and any minimal impact practices that may be in effect specific to that area (such as carrying out waste). Be safe, take care of yourself and the environment, and enjoy the great outdoors!

Exploring Your World

ACA File Photo

The natural world is a complex intricate web. It includes plants, animals, insects, water, flowers, trees, shells, soil, and many other things all interconnected to one another. Outdoor experiences provide a wonderful opportunity for participants to explore their natural world. Participating in activities that teach outdoor living skills not only teaches skills needed to live comfortably in the out-of-doors but also provides an opportunity to learn about what makes up the natural world and incorporates a respect and understanding for the environment. This chapter focuses on how to build on participants' curiosity for the natural world, understanding of the ecosystems, and awareness of our responsibility.

Why Is the Sky Blue?

Children have an innate curiosity for the natural world. Anytime they are in a setting other than what they are used to they want to learn more about it. What they learn will stay with them through adulthood and may even be passed on from generation to generation. Adults, although curious, are typically more reserved and therefore may not be as inclined to participate as children would. Your responsibility as a leader is to encourage that curiosity and provide opportunities for both children and adults to learn.

Getting participants to utilize all of their senses — seeing, touching, hearing, smelling, and tasting — is one of the greatest things you can do to enhance curiosity and help participants gain a better understanding of the environment. For example, on a night hike, participants actually lose their sense of sight due to the darkness, but there is still much learning that can happen. Stop in the middle of a wooded path or park area and have the group stand completely quiet. Ask them what they hear, what they smell, and if they can feel anything around them. The same is true for participants who may be visually impaired. They need to explore their environment using all their senses because their sense of sight is not present.

By using a variety of senses, we can get a complete picture of what things are. We can see how it looks — the size, shape, or color. We can sense what it feels like — if it's soft, rough, fuzzy, or scaly. We can determine what it smells like — if the odor is pleasant or unpleasant. If it's edible, we can taste it and not just determine whether it's sour, sweet, bitter, or salty but also find out what the texture is like. Listening will provide us information on whether something makes noise and what kind of noise it makes — if it's loud, soft, chirping, wailing, rustling. Asking participants to use other senses to explore their world increases their curiosity and makes them more eager to learn. Participants should feel comfortable looking under things, picking things up, and using all of their senses as long as it is not disturbing any natural habitat.

Understanding the Ecosystem

The ecosystem is a complex community of organisms working together to survive or live together in harmony. Everything has a purpose, and understanding the ecosystem will help you understand that everything is interconnected. It's not possible to teach participants everything; however, you can present a few facts that will help them understand the ecosystem and their relationship to it.

Understanding Ecological Principles

Ecology is the study of the interrelations of all plants and animals and their environment. To understand the natural world and to aid participants in exploring their world, we must first look at what ecology is. Ecology studies a combination of LAWS, community, interrelationships, adaptation, the food chain, oxygen and water cycles, and diversity.

The LAWS of Nature

The LAWS of nature are Light, Air, Water, and Soil. Light refers to the amount and intensity of sunlight. Air refers to the quality and temperature of the air. Water stands for the amount and quality of water. And Soil refers to the quantity and types of soil or rocks in the area. All living things — plants or animals — depend on each of these for survival.

Have participants look for different examples of Light, Air, Water, and Soil. An example of a light source is the sun. An example of air would be the wind or blowing up a balloon. Water can be in a lake or in the rain, and examples of soil can be found on the ground as sand or clay soil. Each interacts or interrelates with the others on many levels to form the different environments in which plants and animals live.

ACA File Photo

Community

The LAWS in different combinations make up various communities. Plants and animals live where the environment best suits them, and each plant and animal has a niche or role in that area. For instance, cacti are found in arid and dry regions. This community best suits them. They need very little water and have thick skins to prevent moisture from rapidly transpiring. Cacti would not do very well living in the jungle where it rains a majority of the time; however, they play a crucial role in a desert environment. The roles cacti play include holding soil in place, breaking rocks into smaller pieces, storing water, providing shade, and feeding animals and birds. Certain animal species depend on the cacti for survival and therefore live in the same community. Have participants look around your site and determine what plants and animals make up that community.

Diversity

Each community has a wide range of diversity. Diversity means difference. Just as people differ in size, shape, color, race, religion, background, intelligence, and athletic ability, plants and animals also differ. Diversity has great value in nature. Discuss with your group the different species of plants and animals they might be familiar with. Ask the group to list all the different things they find in their community.

Interrelationships

Everything on earth is connected. In each community, plants and animals interact and coexist. These are known as interrelationships. Each species is an intricate and valuable member with a specific job to do. Animals depend on specific kinds of plants for their food. Some plants shade others, protecting them from the scorching sun; some plants, such as vines, use others for physical support. Each species provides a home for something else, provides nutrients for something, provides moisture for some plant, provides protection for some animal, or provides something for someone.

If we understand that all things are interrelated, we understand that there is a place for everything and everything has its place. To demonstrate this principle, name something (a person, plant, or animal), and ask a participant to name something (another person, plant, or animal) that depends on it. The next person then names something that depends on the previous thing, and so on. Doing so emphasizes interrelationships.

Adaptation

Adaptation is the capability of a plant or animal to change so that it fits the environment. An example of this would be the snowshoe hare, which is brown in the summer and white in the winter to blend in with its environment. Ask participants why the snowshoe hare needs to blend in with its environment (so it is not seen easily by a predator). Another example of adaptation would be nocturnal animals. Some nocturnal animals have larger eyes or bigger ears, helping them to live in a darker environment. Having bigger ears allows them to hear better, and the larger eyes help them to see better even when it is dark. Animals have made these changes so that they can better fit into their community.

Camouflage is another example of adaptation. Some animals that have little protection from predators are colored in such a way that they blend with their surroundings. Their predators then have a difficult time seeing them. Some animals even change colors depending on where they are — a chameleon that can be green when it's on a leaf and brown when it's on a tree is a good example.

Ask participants about some of the adaptations they might make to living in the environment. For example, when it's colder, we generally put on more layers, and if it's bright out, we can put on sunglasses to protect our eyes.

The Food Chain

The food chain is made up of producers and consumers. (Figure 5.1) Producers in the food chain make their own energy. A green plant is an example of a producer. Plants absorb energy from the sun and produce their own energy through a process of photosynthesis. Photosynthesis uses the energy captured from the sun to covert water, carbon dioxide, and minerals into organic compounds, which help the plant grow. Consumers in the food chain eat other things (producers and other consumers) to get their energy. Humans are examples of consumers. We eat foods such as meat, fruits and vegetables, and grains and cereals to give us the energy we need to function and do daily activities. Our bodies do not produce the energy we need to survive; therefore, we need to consume other sources that have the energy we require.

Consumers include herbivores, carnivores, and omnivores. Consumers that eat plants are called herbivores. An example of a herbivore is a cow, deer, or rabbit. Some herbivores are, in

Figure 5.1

turn, consumed by carnivores. Carnivores are consumers that eat meat. An example of a carnivore is a lion or a wolf. If a consumer eats both meat and plants, then it is called an omnivore. Ask participants for examples of omnivores.

Eventually all herbivores, carnivores, and omnivores die and are, in turn, broken down by decomposers. Decomposers break down organic material in plants and animals into basic minerals and chemicals, returning these substances to the soil — where they nourish more plants to produce more energy which, in turn, is eaten by herbivores and omnivores, which are eaten by consumers, and the cycle begins all over again. Discuss with participants where they fit into the food chain.

Cycles

The environment is made up of natural cycles. A cycle is a process with no beginning and no end — it is continuous. Water flows in a cycle, oxygen has a cycle, day and night are cycles, and even the seasons and the tides occur in cycles. All cycles are important, but the two most important cycles include the oxygen cycle and the water cycle.

Oxygen is necessary for the survival of most organisms on earth. Land-bearing animals, which include humans, need to breathe oxygen to survive. We can survive only minutes without oxygen.

As plants use the energy from the sun to photosynthesize (a process in which green plants create a basic energy source), they give off oxygen. When we breathe, we take in oxygen and give away carbon dioxide as a byproduct when we exhale. The carbon dioxide is then in turn used by green plants along with energy from the sun during photosynthesis and gives off oxygen as a byproduct, thus starting the cycle all over again.

The Water Cycle

Three quarters of the earth's surface is covered by water. Of that, 99 percent is found in the oceans; only 1 percent is freshwater, which we need to live. Since a majority of the human body is made up of water, water is essential to human survival. Animals also need water to survive, and plants need water to produce energy. Similar to oxygen, water has a cycle.

Water can be found in three different forms: solid, liquid, and gas. As a solid, water is snow or ice, and liquid water is what you get out of the tap at home. An example of water as a gas is the steam produced from boiling water. Each of these forms is an important part of the water cycle. (Figure 5.2)

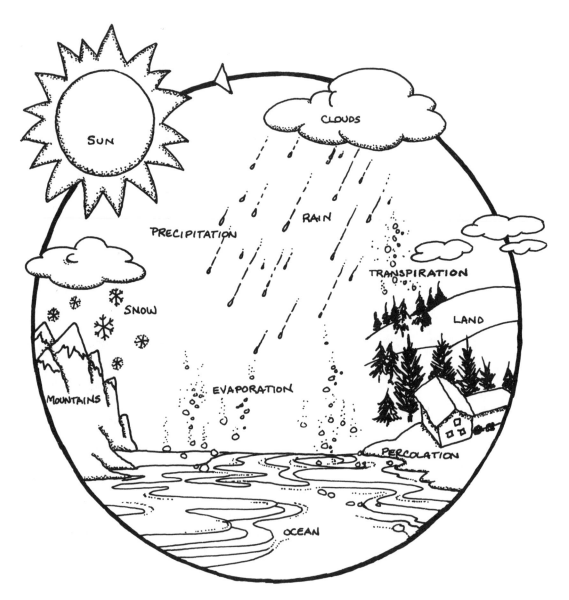

Figure 5.2

What comes to mind when we think of where we find water? Most of the water on the planet is found in lakes, rivers, streams, and oceans. When the sun heats the surface of the water and the energy is great enough to turn liquid into a gas, it evaporates into the atmosphere. Plants also release water into the atmosphere through a process called transpiration. Plants collect water through their leaves and roots and release it through small openings on the undersides of their leaves as vapor. Vapor in the air stays there until it condenses and forms clouds. Condensation happens when evaporated water comes in contact with cold air. A good example of this is the bathroom mirror after a hot shower.

Water vapor will continue to collect in clouds until it is too heavy and falls to earth as precipitation. Precipitation can be in the form of rain, sleet, hail, or snow. When the precipitation hits the earth, it is either collected in lakes, rivers, streams, or oceans or absorbed into the soil through a process called percolation. This is the process in which water is filtered or percolates through the soil.

Helpful Hint

To help remember the process of percolation, imagine an old-fashioned percolating coffee maker. The water comes up through a tube in the coffee pot and is released over the grounds in the basket. The water then percolates or filters through the grounds combining the coffee grounds and water to make the beverage.

Water continues its journey through the soil making its way between soil particles until it reaches the water table, which is essentially an underground river. Any depression in the earth that falls below the water table appears as lakes or ponds.

Understanding Our Responsibility

Now that you have a better understanding of what the environment is and how to help participants explore their world, you also need to understand our responsibility for caring for our natural world and the key role conservation plays. "Conservation" is the future planning and management of an area. It involves programs to promote prudent use and renewal of our natural resources, protecting resources through minimum impact practices and taking the responsibility to improve areas that may have been impacted or devastated by natural or man-made causes.

The premise of conservation dates back to the early nineteenth century in the United States when it became apparent that natural resources were not limitless. After hundreds of years of using natural resources without consideration for future planning, conservation practices employed in Europe finally began to find acceptance in the United States, thus beginning the conservation movement.

Natural and cultural resource management began as early as 1832. Later that century came the protection of Yosemite Valley and the creation of the first national park, Yellowstone. Conservation as a national movement owes much to President Theodore Roosevelt and Roosevelt's first chief forester of the National Forest Service, Gifford Pinchot, who is credited with having first used the term "conservation" in its present context.

Almost 100 years after the beginning of the conservation movement, the federal government developed the Civilian Conservation Corps to preserve and develop the country's natural resources while providing employment and vocational training during the era of the Great Depression. Renowned naturalists and conservationists such as John Muir, Aldo Leopold, and Rachael Carson all understood the value of our natural resources and our responsibility for protecting them and paved the way for conservation through their efforts.

As we continue to use more natural resources in our daily lives, and more people spend greater amounts of time in the outdoors taking advantage of the natural environment for recreational purposes, conservation becomes ever more important. Knowledge of outdoor living skills provides a unique opportunity to give something back to your natural and civic communities while enjoying the great outdoors. Collaborating with agencies such as the U.S. Forest Service, Bureau of Land Management, state departments of natural resources, local parks and recreation agencies, and other conservation organizations allows you to get involved in the resource management of an area.

Projects can include:

* picking up litter;

* educating your local community on recycling;

* making bird houses;

* collecting discarded Christmas trees and installing them as revetments to protect stream banks or submerging them to provide shelter for fish;

* building observation decks and blinds in wildlife refuges;

* developing and maintaining outdoor classroom sites;

* cleaning and repairing statues, gravestones, and other historic monuments;

* restoring historic buildings;

* inventorying significant landmarks and developing documentation to nominate sites to the National Register of Historic Places;

* preparing and presenting research about the people and events important to the heritage of an area;

- assisting archeologists in protecting and studying archeolo sites;

- developing interpretive demonstrations, tours, and living history exhibits in resource areas and helping to present th to visitors;

- increasing accessibility of resource area facilities for disabled visitors;

- upgrading, maintaining, and helping to construct trails for hikers, horseback riders, bicycle riders, and other users;

- teaching environmental awareness skills to young people visiting resource areas;

- providing training in appropriate camping, hiking, and other recreational skills that are easy on the land;

- preparing informational brochures to be distributed at agency visitor centers;

- offering conservation-oriented presentations and slide shows to youth organizations and civic groups; and

- training others in appropriate conservation work skills.

To assist group members in their understanding of responsibility and minimum impact philosophy, it is important to teach them to leave things where they are. Say you are on a hike and come across a pond loaded with tadpoles. This presents an excellent opportunity to talk about the life cycle of the frog. Chances are that many participants have never seen a frog in this stage of life, and some may never have seen a frog up close. As part of this example, you fill a cup with water and collect some of the tadpoles for closer observation. Your participants are so excited that they want to take a few of these critters home and begin filling their cups with tadpoles to transport out and back to the city. Explaining that the tadpoles need to stay in that environment is an excellent opportunity to talk about leaving things as we find them and not removing anything from the environment.

Explain that every species whether it's a frog, plant, or other animal has a specific environment in which they need to live if they are to survive. If you remove the frog from its environment, it cannot survive very long. The argument that there are so many of them that it won't matter may be brought up. Your responsibility as the leader is to help them learn that all things we do in the environment, all the decisions that we make and the actions that we take, no matter how big or small, have an

impact. If everyone who came to the area took only one or two of the tadpoles home, there would be none left to grow into full-grown frogs and begin the cycle all over again. And, taking it one step further, if this species were eliminated, how would that affect the rest of the web?

Teachable Moment

Materials needed: bag of goldfish crackers, red food coloring, sheet or plate, watch with a second hand

Preparation before packing out on your trip:

- Dye about a third of the crackers with red food coloring.

- Allow enough time for crackers to dry.

- Mix the red and regular crackers together.

Activity:

- Spread the crackers on a sheet or plate in an area representing their habitat (pond, lake, etc.) and explain that the habitat represents the area they are currently in (national park, forest, state park, or county forest).

- Count the number of fish on the plate.

- Designate one person from the group to be an eagle, which consumes at least one fish a day.

- Designate at least two people to fish recreationally with a two-fish limit per day.

- Have the remaining participants each take home two fish for their aquariums.

- Let 30 seconds represent one day and then let the participants fish. Tell participants not to eat the fish they have but to hold onto them for the time being.

- Do this until you have just a few fish left (only five or six).

- Discuss the results. How many fish were there at the beginning? How many were left at the end? Would this be enough to sustain the fish population in this habitat? What if more people or predators came to the lake to eat the fish or take them home?

- Discuss the effects of pollution. Ask how many red fish (or contaminated fish) each participant received. Talk about how chemicals sometimes can make fish (or other animals) sick and can contaminate them. The animals (including humans) that

consume too many of these fish will eventually get sick if they eat enough, since by eating the fish they are also consuming the chemicals the fish have in their system. Talk about our responsibility to care for the environment — not just to leave things as we find them (not taking fish for use in the aquarium, catch and release for sport fishing) but also to not pollute the environment with things that might make other animals and organisms sick. Ask participants what they can do to help with conservation efforts that protect the environment.

• Ask for questions.

Summary

Understanding the basics of ecology and our responsibility for protecting the environment is important in learning outdoor skills. Learning about nature and the effect our interactions may have on the environment assists in building sound environmental ethics and respect for the natural world. Practicing conservation continues the tradition of caring for the environment that began well over 100 years ago. The activities in appendix B will serve as a guide for you and participants while you explore your world. Use a few of these activities to help participants understand their world and their role in it.

Putting It on Your Plate

© Claire Steinberg

Cooking outdoors is not as daunting as it seems. Many of the same things you prepare indoors can be done outside; they just require different methods. This chapter will focus on how to plan for meals and the different kinds of food options, heat sources, and methods for preparing them.

Planning Your Menu

So what's for breakfast (and lunch and dinner)? When planning what to eat on your trip, whether it is a simple day hike or an extended overnight trip, you need to consider a number of things. Participating in any outdoor activity will create a healthy appetite, and planning for substantial, satisfying meals is a key to a positive outdoor experience. Meals should be nourishing, satisfying, and revitalizing, but most importantly they should taste good.

Involve participants in meal planning and be aware of any special dietary needs of every member of your group (vegetarians, food allergies, religious considerations). You may want to provide them with a list of suggestions or options from which to choose, or you may allow them complete freedom to plan all the meals for their day or overnight trip, depending on age and experience.

Plan for food that provides enough energy for you to carry out the day's activities. According to the National Outdoor Leadership School, backcountry travelers are estimated to burn between 2500 and 4500 calories daily depending on each person's physiology and activity. Commonly, your caloric intake should consist of 50 percent carbohydrates, 25 percent protein, and the remaining 25 percent fats. These percentages are average, however, and will change depending on the situation. In cold weather, people need a higher percentage of fats than they would during hot weather. Plan for a well-balanced meal that includes the four food groups: meat and fish, dairy, grains and cereal, and fruits and vegetables. (Figure 6.1)

Figure 6.1

Carbohydrates include cereals, grains, pasta, starchy vegetables (such as potatoes and corn), fruits, honey, and flavored gelatin. Proteins are found in meat, cheese, milk, and eggs. Foods with a high content of fat include oil, margarine, butter, nuts, cheese, and meat.

Carbohydrates provide quick energy and are easy to digest. Because this energy doesn't last long, plan into the menu proteins and fats, which require more time and effort to digest but stay with you to provide energy over a longer period of time. When quick and long-lasting energy is needed, such as in cold weather, consider eating oatmeal, dried fruit, or a granola bar.

Good hiking, canoeing, or trip food should be nutritious, simple, easy to prepare, lightweight, compact, inexpensive, nonperishable, and tasty. Plan for three meals a day plus snacks. Serve less per meal than you would at home, eat light, and eat often.

Things to consider in food selection:

• Taste

• Calories

• Ease of preparation

• Nutrition

• Weight and bulk

Other points to consider in menu planning:

• Length of the trip

• Types of activity

• Probable weather conditions

• Availability of water

• Type of stove and fuel

• Number of people to be fed

• Time allotted for cooking

• Cost and variety of the ingredients

Have a good mix of hot and cold meals. At least one meal during the day should be a hot meal. Hot meals are important in cold and rainy weather because they not only help ward off hypothermia but also help refresh and energize the body after a long day. If it's warm, plan a hot meal for the end of the day, and if it's cold, you may choose to have all three meals hot. Use your discretion.

Helpful Hint

A good rule of thumb when determining how much food to bring is to plan on 1 ½ servings per person and to plan food for at least one extra person. Remember that people burn more calories during outdoor activities, so they are bound to eat more.

The planning process may depend on the cost or what's available. If you have a budget or are planning a trip as part of a resident camp or environmental education program, you may be limited to certain foods. Be sure to check with your food service manager to find out what the options are or what can be ordered specifically for your trip.

Packaging

Packaging considerations should include space constraints, the sturdiness of both the packaging and the food item, and preparation time. You can reduce the bulk of most foods by removing them from their original containers and repackaging them in sealable plastic bags or other containers.

Be sure to label all packaged items, including any directions for preparation. For example, suppose that you have both home-made granola and purchased hot cereal. Labeling will eliminate any confusion as to which is which and how to prepare it. Group all the ingredient packets for one meal together in a large plastic bag. In this way, you won't have to search for miscellaneous items. You can also cut the preparation instructions from packaged food items and place them in the bag with the contents.

Safety Tips

- Prepare and store food under safe and sanitary conditions.

- Refrigerate foods that are considered potentially hazardous (those capable of supporting growth of infectious or toxic microorganisms) such as meat, poultry, milk or milk products, fish, shellfish, edible crustacea, and eggs to keep from spoiling. It is recommended that any foods such as these be maintained either at temperatures below 40°F or above 140°F.

- Eat any potentially hazardous foods within the first day of travel.

E. coli and salmonella are two strains of bacteria that can cause serious illness when undercooked or raw meat and eggs are consumed. E. coli infection can cause severe bloody diarrhea and stomach cramps. Be sure to cook all meat to a temperature above 140°F. Salmonella can cause illness associated with eating raw or undercooked eggs. The symptoms are similar to E. coli and include fever, abdominal cramps, and diarrhea. To avoid salmonella, keep all eggs and egg products (such as mayonnaise) refrigerated at a temperature below 40°F.

ACA File Photo

Food Suggestions

Breakfast

Granola, cold cereal, instant hot cereals, bagels, English muffins, dried fruits, cinnamon toast, hot chocolate mix, tea, instant coffee, juice, breakfast bars, breakfast drinks that require water only, pancake mixes that require only water (no eggs or oil), powdered milk, solid or liquid margarine, dried hash browns, freeze-dried eggs, tortillas

Lunch

Rye or whole-grain bread, pita bread or tortillas, crackers, chips, cheeses (string cheese preserves really well), meat sticks or jerky, peanut butter, honey or jelly, instant soups, ramen noodles, raisins and other dried fruits, nuts, bouillon, canned fish, fruits that transport easily such as apples and oranges, carrots, celery, cauliflower, instant drinks

Dinner

Potatoes, fresh and/or dried fruits, instant potatoes, instant soups, macaroni-and-cheese dinners, pasta, rice, instant puddings or other instant deserts, instant sauces, dried herbs, onions, salt and pepper or other spices, dried ice cream, freeze-dried complete meals (usually purchased at a backpacking outfitter), canned chicken or tuna (if weight is not a problem)

It is a good idea to practice all cooking at base camp before trying something new out on the trail. You may find that you want to change the menu, change the ingredients, learn to cook some dishes better, or not take some equipment along on the trip. Prepare in advance any meals that will allow you to do so.

Choosing a Heat Source for Cooking

Even though meals that require little preparation and no actual cooking are easy, it is recommended that you have at least one hot meal a day to help nourish and replenish the body. There are two basic methods for cooking outdoors: camp stoves or open fires.

Unless you are at base camp where there are designated campsites or fire pits, stoves are the preferred method of cooking in an outdoor environment. Although you must take camp stoves with you, they are easy to use, relatively light in weight, and environmentally friendly. Open fires should only be used in a designated area whether that is on camp property, designated campsites on state or federal land, or other areas.

Open fires should never be used where there are no designated sites unless it is an emergency situation.

Camp Stoves

Most camp stoves use an outside fuel source to produce the heat required for cooking. Stoves can be single or double burners. Choosing the right stove for your trip, whether it is short or long, depends on the following factors.

- What kind of trip you will be on

- What kind of meals you will be preparing

- The size of the stove — Does the canister detach? Will it fold together or is it one unit?

- How easy it is to set up

- How long it will burn

- Whether it is sturdy

- How easy it is to light

- How easy it is to control

- How easy it is to maintain

- The type of fuel it uses — The type of fuel you choose will depend on where you are going (high altitude, cold temperature), the weight you are carrying, and how you plan to carry the fuel. If you use liquid fuel, be sure to carry it in a container marked "fuel" so that you do not confuse it with a water container.

Fuel Options for Stoves

A variety of fuels are available, but not all fuel canisters fit all stoves. Be sure to research the stove you have or want to purchase and the type of fuel it uses, and make especially sure that you have the proper fuel containers to fit your stove. Fuels for camp stoves include butane and butane blends, kerosene, white gas, denatured alcohol, and unleaded gas. Many liquid fuel stoves today are dual-fuel stoves and can use a variety of liquids. Be sure to check the manufacturer's instructions to see what fuels are appropriate for your stove.

Butane and butane blends are the safest, easiest, and most convenient to use. Table 6-1 lists some of the pros and cons of camp stoves that use pressurized fuel.

Table 6-1 Camp Stoves and Pressurized Fuel	
Pros	**Cons**
Generally, the safest and easiest to use Fuel comes in a gaseous form, in a pressurized container Can't spill Easy to light Clean burning Easy to regulate, and therefore excellent for cooking many types of foods Easy to pack Don't require messy priming Not as volatile as liquid-gas stoves	Do not work well at high elevations or at temperatures below 50°F Straight butane will not work below 32°F May suffer malfunctions (for example, the knob that turns the stove on and off can get stuck) More expensive than other fuel types Fuel canister must be replaced frequently Fuel canisters are heavier than liquid fuels and their containers

Stoves that use pressurized fuel are an excellent way to teach beginners about camping stoves because they are easy to operate. They are small, easy to carry, and less messy than most stoves.

___

Safety Tip

Be sure to let your camp stove cool down before detaching the fuel canister and packing it with your gear.

___

Cautions for Stove Use

- Always read the manufacturer's directions before using any type of stove.

- There should be little activity around any stove; that activity should be directly related to operating or supervising the operation of the stove.

- Always place these stoves on a level surface to avoid tipping. This will also help to avoid boiling food over the side of a pot.

- Always make sure the fuel canister is seated correctly so that there is no fuel leakage.

- Never put your face over a stove while lighting or operating it.

- Never remove a fuel canister while the stove is on.

- Take enough canisters with you to cover the duration of your trip.

- Always carry empty canisters out with you.

- Do not use stoves inside of a tent where they may tip over and ignite the tent fabric.

- Use stoves 100 feet away from sleeping and water areas.

Open-Fire Sources

Although camp stoves are strongly recommended, open fires may need to be used in emergency situations or if a camp stove is unavailable or breaks down, and there is a designated fire pit. The most common open-fire heat source is charcoal or wood.

Charcoal

Charcoal is wood that has been partially burned so that only the hard fuel remains. It is made from wood that was grown and cut specifically for this purpose. Hardwood charcoal, which burns slowly and generates a lot of heat, is the preferred type.

North Americans tend to use too many briquettes, and the coals keep burning long after the cooking is over, the meal has been eaten, and the area has been cleaned up. Four briquettes are enough to cook hamburgers for two people. Twenty briquettes will cook an entire meal for eight, and you can use the leftover fuel to heat the dishwater.

Starting a Charcoal Fire

Some charcoal is impregnated with an easily ignited material so that it can be lighted with only a match. This type of charcoal may be the easiest to use; however, you'll get a better bed of coals if you use the ordinary kind, which contains no ignition fluid. Ordinary charcoal is more difficult to light and requires some sort of starter.

When using treated charcoal, place the briquettes in a neat pile and light one or more with a match, so that others will ignite from those. After all briquettes are ignited, let the coals sit and heat until the coals give off an orange glow.

Helpful Hint

Whenever you cook over an open fire, soot can collect on the bottom of the pan. To aid in cleanup, rub liquid soap over the outside of the pot. This procedure will make cleaning the black soot off much easier when you're finished cooking.

Nontreated charcoal requires some type of starter. Starter fluids are liquid petroleum products that are sprayed onto the charcoal, allowed to sink in for a minute or two, and then ignited with a match. Because it is a highly flammable liquid, starter fluid is not recommended. You are better off using fire starters to get your fire going.

Before cooking, use a pair of tongs to space the briquettes evenly. A well-controlled bed of coals generates heat at the correct temperature for cooking most foods. After spacing the briquettes, place a metal grate over the coals; then set your pot or pan on the grate. Or, you may place the pot directly on the coals if they have burned down enough.

Fire Starters

A safer, simpler, method of lighting a charcoal fire involves making fire starters. Make a tiny campfire out of tinder, paper, and wood chips, and light that with a match. If you put a small pile of charcoal on top, this little fire will light the briquettes. Small dead sassafras twigs are natural fire starters. Commercial fire starters can also be purchased through companies that deal with camping supplies.

Tin-can Fire Starter

To make a tin-can fire starter, open a tin can (any size from a No. 2 to a No. 10 is appropriate), use the contents, and wash the can carefully. Punch triangular holes in the sides and the bottom with a juice-can opener. Punch similar holes in the sides near the open end. Partially fill the can with charcoal, using four to ten briquettes, and finish filling the can with crumpled paper. Place the can on the ground so that the closed end is at the top, and light the newspaper through the holes you punched at the bottom. The heat from the burning newspaper will be concentrated enough to light the charcoal. When the briquettes are glowing, use a pot-lifter to remove the can. Spread out the charcoal for cooking, or add more briquettes to make a larger, hotter fire.

Fire Starter Cubes

Fire starter cubes can be made from a cardboard egg carton (not a plastic or foam one). Simply fill each egg compartment with small pieces of charcoal and then pour melted paraffin over the charcoal pieces. Pour the paraffin over the briquettes as soon as the paraffin melts, and allow them to dry thoroughly. Later, when you need to start a fire, tear off one of the egg compartments, put it under some briquettes, and light the cardboard, which serves as a wick for the "charcoal candles."

To melt paraffin, follow these steps:

- Place the paraffin blocks in a tin can.

- Place the tin can in a pan of water, essentially making a double boiler.

- Place the pan of water on a stove or fire, and heat the water to a simmer. The hot water will slowly melt the paraffin. Never place a container of paraffin directly over a flame.

- Remove the paraffin as soon as the contents are completely melted.

Newspaper Fire Starters

To make newspaper fire starters, roll strips of newspaper tightly into cylinders about 1 inch thick. Tie the cylinders together with string and dip them into melted paraffin. The end of the string will serve as the wick for this homemade candle.

Tea Lights

Small tea lights, which are candles roughly the diameter of an American half dollar, make a great substitute when you are unable to make your own fire starters. They are small, compact, and travel well.

Wood Fires

When you think of an open fire, wood fires automatically come to mind. For the veteran outdoors person, wood is the ultimate cooking fuel. It can be regulated, is relatively safe, can be used for virtually any type of cooking, and usually can be collected near the campsite. Collecting wood, however, is a trickier matter than it may seem, and may be the greatest drawback to using wood for fuel.

Before you light an open fire, even if there is a designated fire area, be sure to check with local authorities such as the forest or parks service to see if any restrictions are in place for open flames. Building wood fires has been restricted in some areas due to the high fire danger, especially western and southern states.

An alternative to a fire ring is to build a mound fire. A mound of soil 24 inches in diameter is sufficient for a cooking fire. Build a circular mound between 6 and 8 inches high and use this for the base of your fire. Building a fire directly on a large rock is not recommended because it could explode and will leave a visual scar, even if you clean up all the remaining material. Mound fires help to avoid searing the ground below, thus sterilizing the soil that supports plant life. Mound fires can also be easily dispersed after you have finished using them.

After building the mound of soil and laying the fire, place a small, lightweight grate on top. When you use a grate, your fire will burn more evenly and leave less ash, and pans will be less likely to tip over and put out the fire.

Consider taking along a large fire pan and building your fire in that (still on top of the protective layer of mineral soil). This "portable fireplace" will keep the fire contained and the area around it clean.

Gathering Wood

To gather wood, participants should go with a buddy and gather wood within 100 yards from the campsite. They should gather only wood that is dead and has fallen on the ground. They should not break wood off trees even if the trees are no longer living.

Minimum Impact Fact

Gathering wood away from the main campsite keeps the area around the campsite natural.

When gathering wood, participants should collect pieces no thicker than their wrists and should be able to break all pieces by hand. They should gather just enough wood for the group's use and include different sizes.

Three sizes or types of firewood — tinder, kindling, and small fuel — are necessary to build a fire. Tinder includes birch bark, wild grapevines, small sticks, dried spruce, tamarack, pine needles, or other small pieces of wood. Do not pull birch bark off of trees for tinder; use only what you find on the ground. Kindling is larger than tinder between the size of a pencil and an index finger. Small fuel consists of pieces of wood larger than an index finger up to the size of an adult's wrist.

ACA File Photo

Minimum Impact Fact

If you must build a fire in an emergency in a nondesignated area be sure to dismantle and clean the fire area when you leave the site.

Building a Fire

To build a fire, first collect tinder, kindling, and small fuel. The fuel is what actually produces enough heat to cook on. Allow the fuel wood to burn down to coals before cooking. The heat from the coals is much more even than that from the fire. Before beginning, have a bucket or pan of water nearby for extinguishing the fire.

Helpful Hint

To burn fires, you need three things: fuel (wood), air, and a heat source (such as a match). Without a sufficient amount of each, the fire will either not light or go out.

Your cooking fire need not be fancy. Two basic starter fires are the A-frame and the teepee.

An A-frame fire uses a base of three fuel-sized sticks, arranged like the letter A, with the crossbar placed on top of the other two pieces. Put the tinder around the crossbar and then stack the kindling on top. Leave small spaces through which air can move in and out. Put eight to fifteen pieces of kindling on at the beginning so that the heat from the tinder lights the kindling.

To light the fire, strike a match and insert the flame under the crossbar where there is air space. After the match lights the tinder, add it to the fire to serve as another piece of tinder. When the kindling is burning, add small fuel. Remember that a fire needs air to burn. Add fuel and let the fire burn down a bit. Remember that you'll get the best results if you cook over coals instead of flames.

Helpful Hint

A gas lighter typically used for lighting home charcoal grills is good to have along. They last a long time and are also longer so that you can reach farther into the fire set to light it.

To build a teepee fire, place two handfuls of tinder in the center of the fire ring in the style of a teepee. Place kindling around the tinder and then small fuel around the kindling. Be sure to leave space between the wood in order to light the tinder. Teepee fires are effective in that the flame will burn upward fueling the rest of the wood.

When you finish cooking, let the fire burn out. Pieces of trash can be burned as long as they are fully consumed by the fire and turn to ash. Products such as aluminum, steel, and plastic should not be burned at any time. All garbage such as apple cores and other food wastes should be packed out and not burned in the fire.

Helpful Hint

Wood that is "green" or recently fallen or wet will not burn effectively if at all. Choose wood that is dry. If wet wood is your only choice, use a fire starter to assist you in lighting an open fire.

Extinguishing a Fire

To extinguish either a charcoal or wood fire, either let it burn out or sprinkle water on it, a little at a time, until the coals are cold. Make sure that this activity is supervised if working with children or youth. Although it takes more time than just pouring water over the fire, it is less messy and allows the entire fire to cool, not just the top of the coals or wood. Pouring water on a fire also creates steam, which can burn people. Be sure to stir the coals so that all parts are sufficiently cooled. If you used charcoal, you can save the unused portion in a sack for use the next day. Be sure to check with the campsite manager for proper disposal of cool coals. If you are in the backcountry and must use a wood fire, drain the coals, and put the coals into a bucket or sack to dry out so that you can use them again at your next stop or dispose of them in a proper container at the end of the trip. Scatter any remaining ashes throughout a broad area.

Safety Tips

- Water should be available at all times.

- The fire should be no larger than needed.

- NEVER leave a fire unattended.

- Be prepared to put out a grease fire. Salt, flour, and baking powder each will smother a grease fire or remove the air. You can also smother the fire by putting a lid on the pan. NEVER USE WATER TO PUT OUT A GREASE FIRE! Water can spread the fire.

- Be careful of synthetic jackets or pants (windbreakers, running pants, etc.). Embers that land on this material will melt it, which could lead to a serious burn.

Camp Roger, Michigan

- Report all wildfires. NEVER attempt to put out a wildfire. Your first responsibility is to yourself and your group. Remember... safety first!

Minimum Impact Fact

If you have wood left over, scatter it throughout the area; do not leave it for the next group that may come by.

Choosing Cooking Equipment

The type and sizes of cooking equipment depends on the size of the group. A general rule of thumb is to provide each individual with a plate, cup, fork, spoon, and bowl. Bowls can also be used for any food that would be eaten off a plate.

Table 6-2 lists the utensils that each individual camper and each group of participants should take along.

Table 6-2 Camping Cookwear	
Individual Cookwear	**Group Cookwear**

Knife
Fork
Spoon
Plate
Plastic cup
Plastic bowl
Small pot with lid
	Cooking pots with lids (one small and one large to reduce
	   cooking time)
	Frying pan
	Potholder (either the metal pincer type or a
	   hot pad)
	Spatula
	Stove
	Matches or gas lighter
	Fuel
	Biodegradable soap
	Scouring pad
	Can opener
	Strainer
	Plastic containers of salt, pepper, and
	   optional spices
	Backpacker's grill
	Ladle

Helpful Hint

Spices can turn the ordinary into the extraordinary! Sometimes individual packets of salt and pepper, as well as ketchup, mayonnaise, and mustard are very helpful. They last without any refrigeration, can be packed in small plastic bags, and can be individually used.

Packing Out

"Packing out" is a common term used among outdoor enthusiasts. Packing out is simply defined as packing all equipment and material for a trip. Each participant will or should have his or her own pack to use on each trip whether it is a daypack or an overnight extended trip pack. Each person usually carries his or her own gear. For group gear, which can include foodstuffs and cooking supplies, split up the amount you need to carry equally among the members of the group. There should be enough room in everyone's pack to accomplish this.

Cleanup

Doing dishes and cleaning up is a normal part of the process. Participants should wash dishes in a container (wash basin or pot) and not directly in a water source such as a lake or river. Water can be heated over a fire or stove, but be sure to monitor the temperature so that participants do not burn themselves. You may want to pack rubber utility gloves if participants will be putting their hands in boiling water.

All utensils should be cleaned and sanitized after each use. Cleaning dishes will remove the food particles and any residue that might remain. However, to effectively kill any remaining bacteria or other microorganisms that cannot be seen, you need to sanitize all dishes that will be reused. Two methods can help you with this process. The most popular method is to rinse dishes with boiling water. A dip bag (a cheesecloth-type bag) where you place all of your dishes after you have cleaned them, dip them in boiling water, and then hang them to dry is a popular method. A second method is to use a small amount of bleach in the water to assist in killing any unwanted parasites or microorganisms. Check with your local health department for the amount of bleach required to kill any microorganisms.

Helpful Hints

- Wash dishes at least 200 feet from any natural water source.

- Always use biodegradable soap, which is available at back-packing stores and many grocery stores. This kind of soap is not harmful to the environment if it's used in moderation.

- Use as little soap as possible.

- Stay away from natural drainage areas so that soapy water doesn't run back into the lake, stream, or river.

- Take water with you for rinsing dishes away from the stream (remember, 200 feet).

- Be sure to take enough clean water to wash the soap thoroughly from your dishes and silverware. Soap remaining on utensils and dishes can cause diarrhea.

- Strain your dishwater and pack out all remaining food particles.

- Disperse dishwater in a broadcast method. Spread the water out over a large area well away from your main campsite.

Protecting Your Food

The variety of wildlife in the out-of-doors is vast. Depending on the area or country you are traveling in, animals can range from cute chipmunks, squirrels, and rabbits to raccoons, deer, and bears to name a few. Many of these animals usually won't bother you, but some might be interested in the food you are carrying.

In many outdoor areas, a human feeding wild animals either to see them up close or to watch them as they eat is a problem. Feeding wild animals can lead to potential problems as animals become dependent on human food and try to find your food while you are in their environment. In many national parks, bears have been known to break into cars, tents, and trailers to find food that may be left there. Raccoons are infamous for raiding campsites in pursuit of an easy meal.

When camping out overnight, take steps to help prevent animals from getting to your food. Follow these guidelines to ensure the protection of your food.

- Rent or buy bear-resistant portable food containers. Even when you have containers that are bear resistant, be sure to store them away from your main camp area (at least 100 feet).

- If you camp in a main campground area, use the metal box containers that may be available in bear country. These boxes are shared with other campers so be sure to mark your food and bring along additional rope if the containers are full and you need to hang your food.

- Hang your food in a bear bag. Use this option only if the other two methods are not available.

To hang food:

- Find a live tree with a downsloping branch 100 yards from your camping area and at least 20 feet off the ground and 10 feet out from the trunk of the tree.

- Divide your food and aromatic items such as toothpaste, deodorant, sunscreen, bug spray, and lotion into smaller bags (packs work well).

- With a rope that is at least 50 feet long, tie a counterweight (a rock or small branch) to the end of the rope and throw it over the branch at least 10 feet out from the trunk of the tree.

- Tie one bag to the end of the rope, pull it at least 12 feet off the ground, and tie the end securely to the tree.

Helpful Hints

- Cook meals 100 yards away from your site and preferably downwind.

- Hang all food, aromatic items either edible or inedible, and pots, pans, and utensils used in food preparation or consumption in a bear bag, or place in an animal-proof container.

- Avoid wiping hands on clothing and store clothing used for cooking with the food pack.

- Do not allow participants to keep any type of food (including gum and candy) in their tents.

Summary

Meal planning and preparation involves many decisions; what to cook, how to cook it, what kinds of stove and fuel to use, whether to cook over an open fire if stoves are not available, and where and how to store food while on trail. There is no single best way to prepare trip food, so consider where you'll be going, how much you want to spend, how large the group is, how long the trip will last, and what kind of stove or heat source you'll be using. Remember to store your food in a safe place to prevent any animals from having their dinner on you.

Tools and Ties

ACA File Photo

When most of us need to have something repaired or built, we call a service person or go to a store to purchase parts or tools. But when you're practicing outdoor living skills, you probably won't be near either one. It is impractical on a day or overnight trip to take a tool chest, but a few tools and knots are necessary in an outdoor environment.

The only times OLS participants need tools are when they need to repair equipment, prepare meals, or dig a hole for some specific purpose such as a cathole. Ropes, strong cords, and a good selection of knots can take care of most repairs. This chapter is devoted to the tools you'll need and the knots you'll need to know to make outdoor living, cooking, and eating enjoyable, safe, and environmentally sound.

Tool Time

Before the advent of minimum impact practices, many people went into the outdoors with a cache of equipment. Saws, shovels, axes, and hatchets were commonplace to assist in building shelters, gathering wood for campfires, and digging latrines. Today, however, the only tools you will need include a pocketknife, peeler, can opener, and trowel.

Pocketknives

The most common tool — one that everyone should learn to use carefully and safely and one of the ten essential items — is the pocketknife or jackknife. Many types of knives are available and range in a variety of sizes from small utility knives to larger bowie knives. Pocketknives, however, are compact, yet big enough and strong enough for tasks requiring sturdy blades. Experienced outdoors people use two kinds of pocketknives: a knife with one or two blades and a knife with four blades (one cutting blade, a combination bottle opener and screwdriver, a can opener, and an awl or another cutting blade — Figure 7.1).

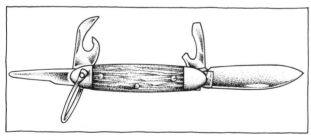

Figure 7.1

Other tools that may be part of a pocketknife include a corkscrew, a saw, a Phillips screwdriver, a toothpick, tweezers, scissors, and even a magnifying lens.

The main reason for selecting a relatively small knife is ease of use. Your pocketknife should fit into your pocket securely and in

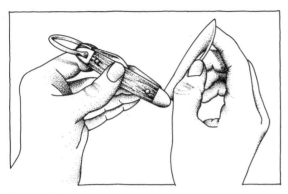

Figure 7.2

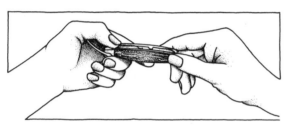

Figure 7.3

your hand comfortably. If it doesn't fit comfortably, it's too big. It should be made of good-quality steel, fashioned so that the cutting blades stay sharp. Look for a knife that has a textured handle (such as bone, staghorn, or textured plastic) or a strong plastic handle (such as the well-known Swiss Army knife).

To open a pocketknife, hold it in one hand, pinching it between the thumb and fingers or the base of the thumb and the tips of the fingers, and insert the thumbnail of your free hand into the slot in the knife blade. (Figure 7.2) Don't move the hand you're holding the knife in until the blade is all the way open.

To close the knife, reverse the process. Be sure to hold the handle between the base of the thumb and the tips of the fingers so that no part of your hand is near the slot into which the blade will fit. (Figure 7.3) A good knife closes with a snap caused by a fairly tight spring. If your fingers are in the way, the knife could cut them as it snaps shut. Always remember...safety first!

Practice opening and closing several pocketknives to find one that feels comfortable and is easy to use. Then practice opening and closing the other tools on the knife.

Safety Tip

If you're using a knife that has a screwdriver, can opener, and awl, practice with the screwdriver first. It's the tool that's least likely to cut you if you close it incorrectly.

Of course, only youngsters who are capable of following directions — and of understanding the importance of keeping their fingers away from the slot in the handle — should be taught how to use a pocketknife. Also, young children probably won't have the fine motor skills it takes to open and close a pocketknife. An adult should supervise the use of knives at all times.

Although the pocketknife is one of the most common tools, it's also the one that causes the most injuries. Always use the knife properly, and when finished, close the knife and put it away. Never run or walk around with an open knife.

Using a pocketknife is relatively safe if you follow one simple, never-to-be-broken rule. Keep your thumb off the back of the blade. Pressure on the back of the blade causes it to close, so putting any pressure on the back of the blade is dangerous. A skilled knife user holds a knife with his or her fingers around the handle so that the thumb is on the index finger.

When you use a knife, hold your elbows against your sides to keep the knife from moving farther from your body than the hand and wrist can move. You'll get better leverage, strength, and control if you regulate the distance in which the blade travels by holding your arms snugly against your sides.

Practice using a nonfolding knife to cut the loop of a doubled-over piece of string. Hold the string in one hand so that a small loop hangs in front of you; hold the knife in your other hand. Cut the string by pushing the sharp edge of the blade against the string, pushing the blade away from your body. Try cutting rope, a piece of meat or vegetable, or anything else that will help you get comfortable with using the knife. Always push the blade away from your body. Be sure to keep your elbows in so that the knife won't make a large arc and cut someone standing nearby.

Before you pass a knife, close it first if you are able to do so (some knives such as cooking knives have fixed blades, which means they don't open and close). If you need to pass a knife with an open blade, hold the back of the blade between the base of your thumb and fingertips, cutting edge facing the ground, so that the receiver can grasp the handle. Always pass a knife slowly, making sure that the receiver has a good grip on it before you let go. Never put your fingers under the blade, or they could be cut as the receiver pulls the knife from your hand.

If you need to put a knife down so that you can do something else, either leave it open on a cutting board, or close it (but be sure to clean it before you close it). Never leave an open knife where someone might sit on it, stumble on it, or run into it.

When you finish using the knife, make sure that it is clean and dry before you put it away. Your knife may occasionally need a drop of lightweight machine oil to keep the hinge free of dirt and rust.

Some knives have a cord or metal loop on the handle. Tying a rope, such as parachute cord, to the loop or cord and then to your belt or belt loop will prevent the knife from dropping out of your pocket. Tying a knife to your belt is better than attaching it to your belt loops because the loops often tear; however, use the loops if you aren't wearing a belt. A good way to tie a knife to your belt is to make a bowline (see instructions later in this chapter) in the end of the cord and slip it over the belt, and then slip the other end of the rope through the bowline and pull it tight. If the bowline is bigger than the pocketknife itself, you can keep the knife tied to the other end and simply slip the knife in and out of the bowline when you want to remove it. Keep the rope free from the knife blade when you are closing it. Also, be sure that the cord is long enough that the knife will fit easily into your pocket while it's attached to your belt.

Cooking Tools

Two cutting tools — the paring knife and the peeler — are especially useful when preparing meals whether on an extended overnight trip or on a short day hike where they are required for meal preparation. A can opener is also an important item.

Paring Knife

A paring knife is used to pare or peel potatoes, apples, and other fruits and vegetables and to cut them into small pieces. Use a paring knife just as you would a pocketknife, but add one additional skill.

Usually, people pare (peel) toward themselves, rather than away. Because the skin of most fruits and vegetables is thin and the objects themselves are small, you'll be most successful if you learn to peel apples, potatoes, carrots, and other foods by carefully moving the knife toward you.

Hold the knife in the hand you use for cutting and the object to be pared in the other hand. Holding your elbows close to your body, lay the knife handle across the base of the fingers of the knife hand, with the blade extending beside your thumb. Close your fingers around the handle.

Now hold the knife against an apple or potato and push against the apple or potato with your thumb while you move the blade across the peel and above the side of your thumb. The lower part of the fingers holds the knife handle and moves it toward the palm. Push the apple or potato with the thumb, and move the knife with your fingers and palm. This process is tricky at first, but once you learn it, paring will be as easy as riding a bicycle. Always exercise good judgment and caution when using any knife.

Safety Tip

Adults should supervise children when they are using paring knives.

Peeler

The peeler, which is used in the same way as a paring knife, is really easier to use because the guide on the back of the peeler prevents the user from cutting off too much of the apple or potato. Many peelers are made to go forward or backward. When peeling something long, such as a carrot, you have the choice of pushing the peeler away from you or pulling it toward you, or alternating. As you do with a knife, be sure to keep the fingers that are holding the object below the object so that only it will be peeled.

Figure 7.4

Can Opener

Because many types of can openers are available, the only kind explained here is the pocketknife can opener, which is often a curved blade resembling a hook. (Figure 7.4) To use this type of can opener, place the curved part (the bottom of the hook) outside the rim on the top of a can and the sharp blade part (the top of the hook) inside the rim, running parallel to it. Using the hook, press against the outside of the can while lifting the knife handle. The blade inside the rim will move into the can top and make a small cut in it. Move the hook forward and lift the handle again. Keep repeating this movement until you've gone all around the can. This will take some time. Remember to keep the bottom part of the opener blade tight against the outside of the rim of the can and to lift slowly at first. Be aware of the sharp edge of the lid and the can — either can cut fingers very easily.

Sharpening Knives

Knives must be kept sharp at all times. To sharpen a knife, you need a sharpening stone or a whetstone. A whetstone must be moistened with either water or oil to keep the knife moving freely and to prevent the blade from becoming too warm. A whetstone usually has a rough side and a smooth side. The rough side removes nicks and very dull edges; the smooth side hones the blade to a truly keen edge.

Hold the moistened or oiled whetstone in one hand, being sure to keep your fingers below the top edge so that the knife won't cut them. Place the knife, blade down flat on the top of the stone, and then raise the back of the blade at a slight angle

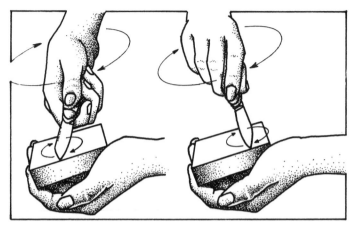

Figure 7.5

(about 15 to 20 degrees). Pull the blade across the stone, leading with the sharp edge. The back edge should never touch the stone. Stroke the blade across the stone, and after a few strokes, make circular strokes as you pull the blade across. After a few more strokes, turn the knife over and sharpen the other side. Keep this up, alternating sides, until you think that the blade is smooth. Be sure to sharpen the entire blade, from base to tip. (Figure 7.5)

To test the blade, cut some wood or rope. If the knife seems sharp, finish the job by stroking the blade across the smooth side of the stone a few more times to remove any rough edges.

Digging Tools

Digging tools are needed for making a toilet, and you may use them to clear out a fire pit to pack out burned material. If you will be camping or hiking away from existing toilet facilities, bring a trowel. A trowel is a small shovel commonly used in gardening. Trowels should be kept clean and relatively sharp. To keep them rust-free, wipe them with a rag bearing lightweight machine oil after cleaning.

Many backpackers use a trowel made of Cycrolac, a hard, lightweight plastic that withstands rugged use. Cycrolac is lighter than metal and doesn't bend the way inexpensive lightweight metal does. Furthermore, it doesn't get rusty. See chapter 4, "Being Safe," for information on digging a cathole or latrine.

Knots and Hitches

Almost everyone is familiar with how to tie a basic knot. We use knots every time we tie our shoes. But now, with the invention and use of such products as velcro, buttons, snaps, and pre-made gift bows, we don't really pay attention to how to tie knots.

Imagine replacing a broken shoelace five miles from home, or trying to keep your tent from falling down and blowing away without any knowledge of how to tie it securely. Will your canoe drift away because you didn't secure it tightly? Can you put up a clothesline? Can you make simple repairs to your equipment without the use of knots? Knots are an important part of outdoor-living skills for exactly these reasons. Knowing how to tie a few knots can be the difference between a successful trip and a miserable one.

The difference between knots and hitches is simple: knots (at least the ones you will learn here) are easy to tie, are permanent fastenings until they're untied, and are easy to untie. Hitches are temporary fastenings that can be undone easily and quickly. This chapter includes thirteen of the most popular and most useful knots and hitches.

Knots and hitches can be tied with twine, cord, or rope made of natural or synthetic materials. The advantages of synthetic materials, such as nylon and plastic, are that they do not rot easily, are not affected by water, and stretch only under pressure. Some synthetics, however, are stiff and hard to tie, particularly the plastic cord used for clotheslines. Natural fibers, which are more fragile than synthetics, may shrink, stretch, or rot when wet, but they are generally easy to tie.

You may find that "parachute cord" — a fairly small, flexible nylon rope — is the best for your everyday needs. If so, you may want to include 25 to 50 feet of it in group gear. It can be cut into shorter lengths if necessary. Parachute cord makes a good clothesline, is strong enough to secure large items, and will last for many years.

Tying Knots

When learning or teaching others how to tie knots, use a standard language so that everyone knows what parts of the rope you are referring to. The following are the terms you need to know and use.

Definitions for Knot Tying

- Working end or free end — the part of a rope you are working with

- Standing end — the rest of the rope; the part of the rope you are not working with, whether it is 12 inches or 100 feet long

- A bight — (rhymes with "bright") a bend in the rope

- A loop — the configuration made when you cross one part of the rope over another part

- Overhand loop — the configuration made when you cross the free end over the standing end

- Underhand loop — the configuration made when you cross the free end under the standing end

ACA File Photo

Preparing a Rope

When you buy a rope, bind the ends so that no unraveling occurs. Nylon rope can be melted so that it won't unravel, but this should only be done by an adult. Simply touch a burning object, such as a match, to the end of the rope. As soon as the strands are melted together, dip the end into water.

Safety Tip

Be sure to melt nylon rope outdoors, and be careful that you don't inhale the fumes, which are poisonous. Also, take care not to drip melted nylon on anyone or anything as it is very hot and will burn skin or fabrics.

To bind natural materials or rope you don't want to melt, you can tape or whip the end with a smaller rope. This method, however, is not permanent. A better method is to tie a knot in each end. These knots are called stopper knots.

Stopper Knots

There are two kinds of stopper knots: the overhand knot and the figure-eight.

Overhand Knot

To prevent the end of a rope from unraveling, tie an overhand knot using the following steps:

1. Make a loop in the end of the rope, and push the free end in and out of the loop. (Figure 7.6)

2. Pull the rope tight and you will have an overhand knot. (Figure 7.7)

3. Practice tying the knot close to the end of your rope. If you can pull the knot out by tugging on it, you tied it too close to the end.

Figure 7.6

Figure 7.7

Figure 7.8

Figure Eight Knot

Tying a figure eight involves one more step than the overhand knot, but this knot holds tighter and prevents the rope from unraveling longer. (Figure 7.8) To tie a figure eight, follow these steps:

1. Make a loop in the end of the rope, just as you did for the overhand knot.

2. Pass the free end of the rope once around the standing end and back on top of itself before you push it through the loop.

3. Pull the free end tight to secure the knot.

Whipping a Rope

You can also prevent unraveling by whipping a rope. The term "whipping" means wrapping a piece of twine or smaller rope around the end of the rope. The twine must be wrapped neatly and tightly and must not slip off the rope when you pull on it.

Whipping ropes is a good activity to practice when sitting in a park, talking on an overnight, or any other time you can find the time. It takes time and patience to master.

To whip a rope, follow these steps:

1. Make a bight in a piece of twine or smaller rope that is about 12 inches long. Lay the bight on the rope so that both ends (free and standing) are toward the end of the rope to be whipped. The free end of the twine should be hanging off the end of the rope. (Figure 7.9)

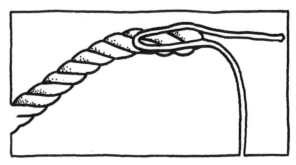

Figure 7.9

2. Holding the bight with your finger, wrap the standing end around both the twine and the rope, toward the bight itself. Be sure to leave the free end of the twine hanging out. Make the wrapping neat; don't let any wrap cross a previous wrap. Be sure to keep winding the twine tightly against the previous turn. Whippings must be precise, even, and smooth so that the windings won't catch on anything. (Figure 7.10)

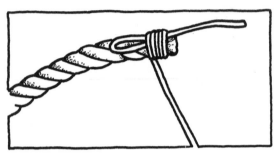

Figure 7.10

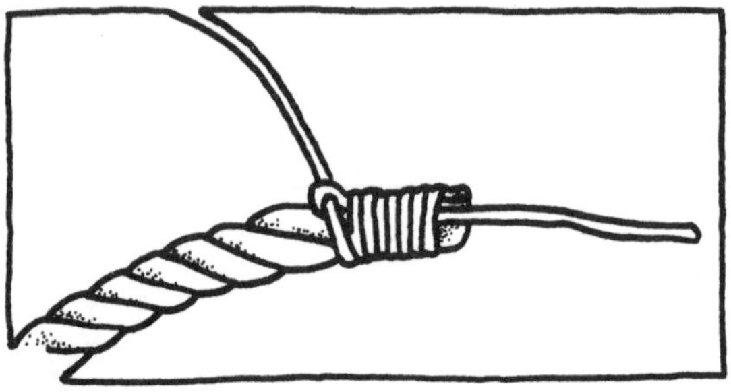

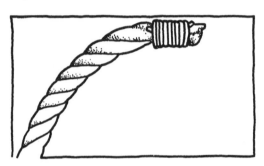

Figure 7.11

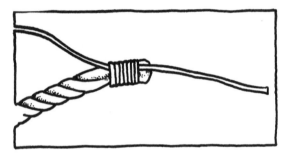

Figure 7.12

Figure 7.13

3. After you have whipped about 1 inch around the rope, slip the end of the twine through the bight (which should still be sticking out), and, holding tight, pull on the free end. (Figure 7.11)

4. Pull the twine until the bight disappears into, and goes about halfway down inside, the length of the wrapping. (Figure 7.12)

5. Cut off the dangling ends. (Figure 7.13) The length of a whipping is usually the same as the diameter of the rope being whipped.

Joiner Knots

As the name suggests, joiner knots are used to join two pieces of rope, cord, or twine. Joiner knots include the square knot and the sheet bend, which are essential outdoor living skills. Other joiner knots include the double sheet bend, the bow knot, the granny knot, the slip knot, the fisherman's knot, the surgeon's knot, and the carrick bend, but they are not covered in this book.

Square Knot

The most useful knot of all may well be the square knot. It is used to join two pieces of rope, twine, or cord, each of equal thickness. It is also one of the strongest knots.

You can practice tying square knots with two pieces of rope or cord of equal thickness or with one piece of rope. A square knot is used to repair a shoelace or to tie around something such as a package or branch. To tie a square knot, follow these steps:

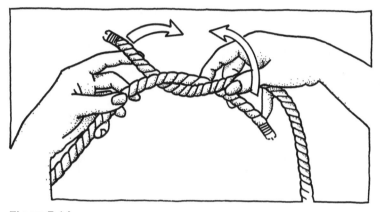

Figure 7.14

1. Hold one end in each hand. Cross one end over the other, then around behind, underneath, and back up in front of the other. (Figure 7.14)

2. Using the same end (it is now in the other hand), cross it over the other, around behind, underneath, and back up in front of the other. (Figure 7.15) Essentially, you are doing the same thing that you did in the first step, only backwards.

3. Pull tight, and you have a square knot. (Figure 7.16)

Figure 7.15

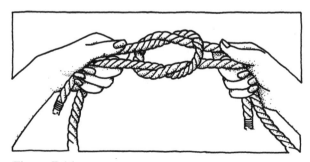

Figure 7.16

An old rule says, "Right over left and under; left over right and under." Try left over right and then right over left; you can start with either the right or the left end; it doesn't make any difference. You can use this saying or come up with another the entire group remembers.

Sheet Bend

If the two pieces to be tied together are of different thicknesses, a modified square knot called the sheet bend is used. This knot prevents the smaller rope from sliding out. To tie a sheet bend, follow these steps:

1. Make a square knot, but don't pull it tight. (Figure 7.17)

2. Cross the working end of the thinner rope over its standing end, and tuck it down through the loop of the thicker rope. (Figure 7.18)

3. Pull the rope tight. The extra turn of the thinner rope will hold the knot in place. (Figure 7.19)

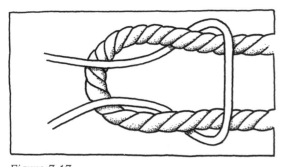

Figure 7.17

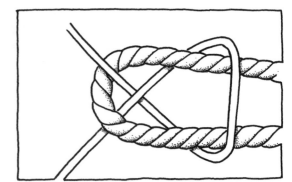

Figure 7.18

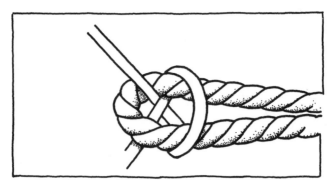

Figure 7.19

Tying Hitches

There are many different kinds of hitches, including the slippery, timber, rolling, chain, marlin spike, midshipman's, and tiller's hitch. This book is concerned only with the most common hitches: the clove hitch, the half hitch, the bowline hitch, and the tautline hitch.

Clove Hitch

A clove hitch is used to fasten a rope to a tree, post, or similar object when there will be a steady pull on the rope as with a clothes line. (Figure 7.20) Because a clove hitch will slip if it is not kept taut, it is not used to secure moving objects, such as a boat or an animal (for example, a horse). To tie a clove hitch, follow these steps:

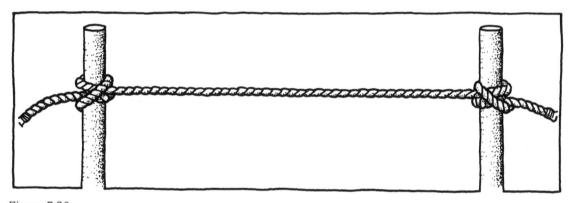

Figure 7.20

1. Pass the free end of the rope behind the post.

2. Bring the free end around to the front of the post and cross the standing end, making an X. (Figure 7.21)

3. Pass the free end behind the post again, below the X.

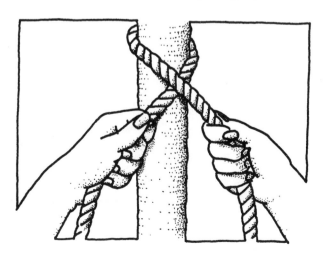

Figure 7.21

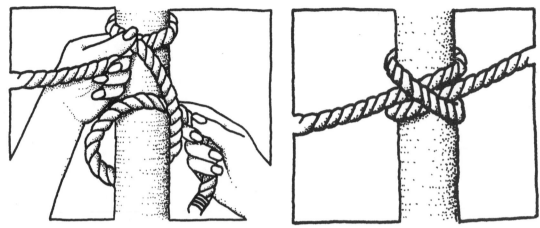

Figure 7.22   Figure 7.23

4. As you bring the free end around to the front of the post again, pass it under the X so that it comes out between the previous two turns around the post. (Figure 7.22)

5. Pull both ends tight. Be sure to pull the free end directly opposite the standing end — if you pull one part out at a right angle to the other, the hitch won't hold. (Figure 7.23)

Half Hitch

Half hitches are tied at the ends of ropes holding boats or horses to rings or poles. A couple of half hitches tied in the ends of a cord used for tying square knots adds security. To tie a half hitch, follow these steps:

1. Pass the free end of the rope behind a pole or through a ring and around to the front again, and then pass it under the standing end. (Figure 7.24)

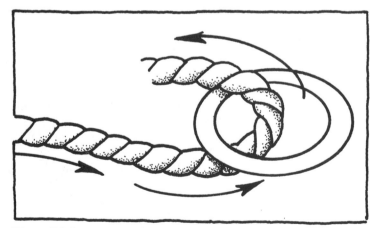

Figure 7.24

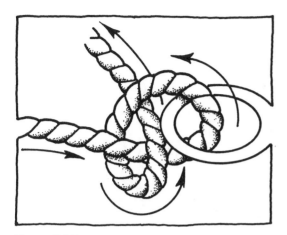

Figure 7.25

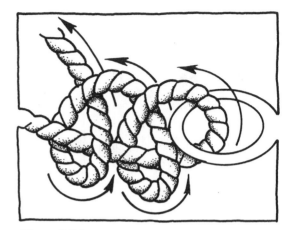

Figure 7.26

2. Bring the free end up and in front of the standing end and then tuck it into the bend. (Figure 7.25)

3. Make another half hitch on the standing end of the rope, away from the ring or post. (Figure 7.26)

Now, you have two half hitches, which make a sliding knot. The two half hitches can be moved up and down the standing part of the rope. They will not hold firmly unless they're snugly against the pole or ring.

Bowline Hitch

At times you'll need a loop that won't slip into a smaller or larger size. The bowline (pronounced bowl'n) is the knot to use. To tie a bowline hitch, follow these steps:

1. Holding the rope in one hand, make a small (4-inch-diameter) overhand loop about 12 inches or more from the free end. The length of rope from the overhand loop to the free end should be a little longer than the circumference of the loop that you want to create. (Figure 7.27)

Figure 7.27

Figure 7.28

Figure 7.29

Figure 7.30

2. Pass the end of the rope around something like a log, pole, or metal ring to make this larger loop. (Be sure that the small loop you made is an overhand loop.) (Figure 7.28)

3. Hold the overhand loop with one hand and, with the other hand slip the free end of the rope through the overhand loop from behind. Pass it around behind the standing end, and back down into the original overhand loop. (Figure 7.29 and Figure 7.30)

Teachable Moment: Keys to making bowlines

To teach the bowline to beginners, you could call the free end of the rope the rabbit and tell the participants to make a hole (loop) for the rabbit. The rabbit comes out of the hole, runs around behind the tree (standing end), and goes back down into the hole.

- Be sure that the first loop is an overhand loop.

- Be sure that the free end goes into the overhand loop from behind and comes toward you.

- The free end then goes around behind the standing end and back down into the original overhand loop.

- Practice, practice, practice.

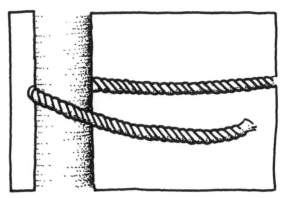

Figure 7.31

Tautline Hitch

Everyone using a tent should learn the tautline hitch, which regulates the tension (tightness) of the lines that hold the tent and/or rain fly to the tent stakes. Sometimes, it may be necessary to use lines other than the ones that come with the tent. In such a case, you will need to tie a tautline hitch. It's easiest to tie a tautline hitch if you tie it to something. To tie a tautline hitch, follow these steps:

1. Tie one end of a piece of rope 2 or 3 feet long to a fixed object (a tree or other stationary object) with two half hitches.

2. Push a tent stake or a stick into the ground about two-thirds of the length of the rope away.

Helpful Hint

Make sure that the tent stake or stick is angled slightly away from the fixed object as you push it into the ground.

---

3. Pass the end of the rope around the tent stake and pull it fairly tight so that it won't slip off. (Figure 7.31)

4. Make two or three overhand knots around the standing end and toward the tent stake. (Figure 7.32 and Figure 7.33)

Figure 7.32

Figure 7.33

Figure 7.34

5. Make another overhand knot around the standing end toward the fixed object. Pull this knot tight. (Figure 7.34)

6. You can pull on the tautline hitch and slide it up toward the fixed object. If you use this hitch on a tent or tent fly, you'll be able to hold the tent tight because the hitch won't slip back until you pull it back.

Summary

You have just learned about knots, hitches, and whipping, which are basic knots for outdoor-living skills. There are approximately 75 simple knots and hitches and up to 8000 intricate ones. Take the time to learn other intricate knots that might help you out on trail, but don't forget the simple knots learned here.

Finding Your Way

ACA File Photo

"Second star to the right and straight on 'til morning." Finding his way to Neverland was not a problem for Peter Pan, but Wendy, John, and Michael had to stop and ask for directions. How many times have you asked yourself, "Which way do I need to go"?

Finding our way is an everyday occurrence whether it's walking to school, driving to work, taking the back roads on vacation, or just strolling down the street. If we don't know how to get there, we need to find out by asking for directions or checking a local map. In urban and even rural areas, street signs, addresses, and even buildings or other structures (natural or man-made) help us find our way. The outdoors is also filled with such markers as streams, lakes, hill tops, and mountains to help us find our way. Special maps help us navigate through the out-of-doors; they show us where we are, the area we are traveling in, the destination we want to reach, and the layout of the landscape. However, a map will only get us so far. To really find our way in the outdoors, we need to use a map and a compass. A compass will show us the direction we want to go and help us keep our bearing while on trail. This chapter focuses on the use of a map and compass, how to read both, and how to use them together.

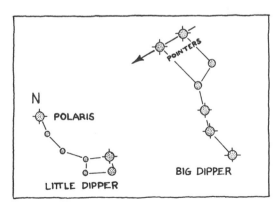

Figure 8.1

To get a rough idea of direction, nature offers some wonderful, easy-to-remember direction indicators. For example, if you face the rising sun, you are facing east, and north is on your left side. If it's evening, the sun is in the west. On a starry night, you can find north by locating the Big Dipper and the two stars that make up the end of its bowl. (Figure 8.1) These two stars are pointer stars. If you draw an imaginary line from the bottom of the bowl to the top and extend it, the first star your extended line will touch is the North Star, or Polaris. (Polaris is also the last star in the handle of the Little Dipper.) As the earth rotates, the Big and Little Dippers rotate around the North Star.

Maps

Maps are wonderful tools for finding buried treasure, locating lost mines, and traveling to strange places without getting lost. Maps have been in use for thousands of years. The earliest known evidence of map use dates back to 1000 B.C. Babylonia. Maps are essential for finding our way.

In its simplest form, a map is a picture of something seen from above. If you draw a picture of the top of your desk, with all the items on it in their proper places, you have drawn a map. Try drawing a map of your own. Pretend that you're in a helicopter or airplane, and draw what you would see when you look down at a playground, a churchyard, your school, your camp, or any other small area.

A map of any land area serves two basic purposes:

- It helps us establish our bearings or directions of travel, in the area represented by the map.

- It helps us orient ourselves through triangulation. "Triangulation" means finding two visible landmarks, noting our relative position to them (the observer and the two landmarks make the three points of a triangle), and then locating that same relative position (the same triangle) on the map.

The following sections describe the two major types of maps you'll probably use — planimeteric and topographic.

Planimetric Maps

A "planimetric map" is a drawing of the land as it would appear if it were as flat as the top of a table, and it indicates distance between the places on the map. (Figure 8.2) The highway map used to route a path from one city to another or across the country is a planimetric map because the roads, highways, and cities are drawn as though they were flat. The area represented by the map has hills and valleys, but they are not important on this type of map (a topographic map does that job); all the planimetric map shows is a drawing of the roads and highways, with their names or numbers, where they go, and how far it is between cities.

Topographic Maps

"Topography" is the study of the land and the natural and man-made objects on it. A "topographic map" is a drawing of the

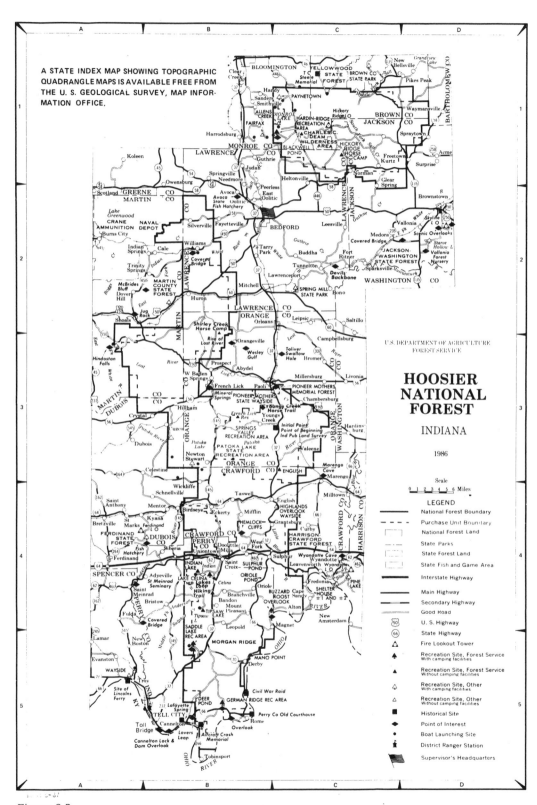

Figure 8.2

Figure 8.3

land and man-made objects. Most outdoor participants call these maps "topo" maps, for short. (Figure 8.3)

Topo maps contain contour lines that show the locations of hills and valleys, as well as how steep, high, and low they are. Each contour line is given an elevation and the closer the lines are to one another, the steeper the incline. This information is especially useful to hikers who want to know how steep the hills along a certain route are; if the hills are too rugged, they might choose to select an easier route.

In the backcountry or on any hiking trail, knowing the contour of the land is very important in determining your travel plans. Some hiking trails follow deer or elk routes, and those routes can be very steep or go through areas you may not want to go through. A topo map will give you an idea of the landscape and help you steer clear of areas you may not want to hike in.

How to Get a Topo Map

Topographical maps of nearly all the United States are available from the Office of the U.S. Geological Survey (often referred to as USGS) and can be found on the Internet at www.mcmcweb.er.usgs.gov/topomaps. To order maps, use one of the following options:

- Refer to your local phone book's yellow pages for the nearest commercial dealers that sell USGS maps or a local outfitter and contact them directly for pricing and ordering information.

- The Web page titled "Finding and Ordering USGS Topographic Maps" offers several methods to locate and order maps. The address is www.mac.usgs.gov/mac/findmaps.html.

- For more information or ordering assistance, call 1-888-ASK-USGS (1-888-275-8747), contact any USGS Earth Science Information Center (ESIC) at www.mapping.usgs.gov/esic/esic_index.html, or write:

    USGS Information Services
    Box 25286
    Denver, CO 80225

The Web site lists all map dealers that sell USGS topo maps across the United States. This site also has a link to map dealers around the world. When you write to the USGS, ask for a map index of the state you're interested in, a topographic map symbols sheet, and an order form. When the index comes, you'll see that each state is divided into rectangles called quadrangles. Select the quadrangles you want maps of, and fill out your order form accordingly.

Other sources include the U.S. Forest Service and the National Park Service. Both agencies have developed planimetric and topographical maps of many of the areas that they administer. Many cities have map companies that deal in all types of maps. Some backpacking or outdoor equipment stores have topo maps of the area's trails.

Contour Lines

Topo maps are relatively easy to read. Contour lines show elevation changes on land and water. Contour elevation changes can be 20, 40, or 80 feet, with every fifth line drawn heavier than the others. You can easily determine the elevations by reading the numbers listed on the heavy lines and adding or subtracting 20, 40, or 80 feet for each of the lighter lines between them. On maps with 20-foot contour intervals, the elevation difference between dark lines is 100 feet; on maps with 40-foot contours, the difference is 200 feet; and on maps with 80-foot contours, the difference is 400 feet. Contour intervals are listed at the bottom of USGS topographical maps.

Note the difference between a topographical map with 40-foot contours and one with 80-foot contours. The map that has contour lines with 40-foot intervals has more detail than the one with 80-foot intervals.(Figure 8.4)

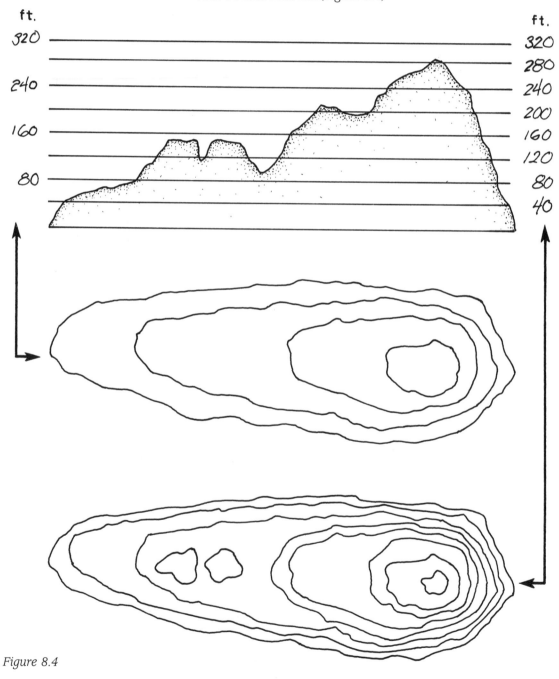

Figure 8.4

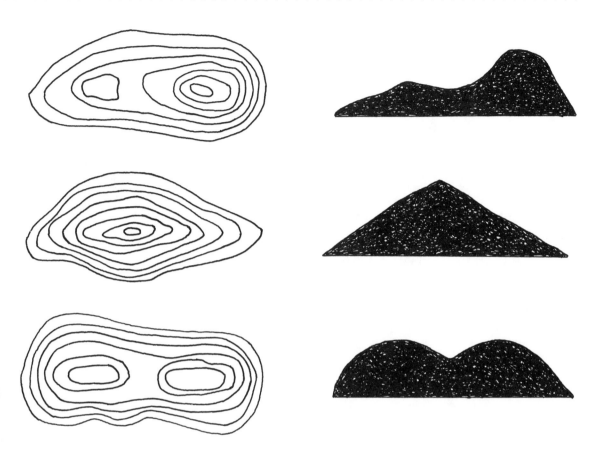

Figure 8.5

Here the shapes of various hills are depicted by contour lines. (Figure 8.5)

Learning to read contour lines will help you determine how the land rises or descends and how steep it is. The closer together the contour lines are, the steeper the land is. The figure on page 156 shows that the land rises to more than 12,000 feet; this map obviously came from a state that has elevations above that height. In the example, the contour lines are 40 feet apart, and there is a difference of 200 feet of elevation from one dark line to the next. The highest point is 12,212 feet. Can you find it?

Symbols

Symbols on a map help identify man-made structures (cultural features), water (hydrographic features), plant life (vegetation features), and elevation (hypsographic features). Some examples of the symbols for these features are shown here. These examples are taken from the USGS topographic map symbol sheet. Look at the examples and locate the symbols for trail, footbridge, school, buildings, and spring. Most of the symbols on a map look like the things they represent. On a U.S. Geologic Survey map, contour lines for land are brown and those for water are blue; areas covered by vegetation are green; and rocks, glaciers, and snowfields are white.

Many topo maps have the following features listed in the margin: (Figure 8.6)

- The name of the map is printed in the top right corner and the bottom right corner of each map.

- The age of the map, or the date when the map was printed, is listed under the map name in the bottom right corner. If the map is old, it may not show recent changes in man-made structures, such as trails and roads. Supplementary maps that show the new structures may be necessary.

- The scale of the map, or the actual distance represented by an inch or other measurement, is written somewhere on every map. A planimeteric map may list the scale in a box titled "Map Explanation" or "Legend." On a USGS topo map, the scale is listed at the bottom of the map. This scale will be 1:24,000, 1:62,500, or 1:250,000. The scale 1:24,000 means that one inch on the map equals 24,000 inches, or 2000 feet in the field.

Maps drawn to the scale of 1:62,500 are most commonly used by hikers and canoeists. This scale is very close to being 1 inch to 1 mile. (There are 63,360 inches in a mile, so 62,500 is close enough for most purposes.) This scale is used for almost all topo maps in the United States.

The scale 1:250,000 is equal to about 1 inch for every 4 miles. Maps drawn to this scale are good mainly for locating points of interest within 100 miles.

Fun Fact

There are 5280 feet in a mile. Did you ever wonder why we use such an odd number? During the days of the Roman Empire, someone determined that the average pace (two steps) of a Roman soldier was 5.28 feet, and that when a soldier had taken 1000 paces (double steps), he had traveled *milia passuum* — Latin for one thousand paces (or 1000 times 5.28). In English, that phrase was shortened to mile. So, if you walk 1000 paces, you have walked close to 1 mile.

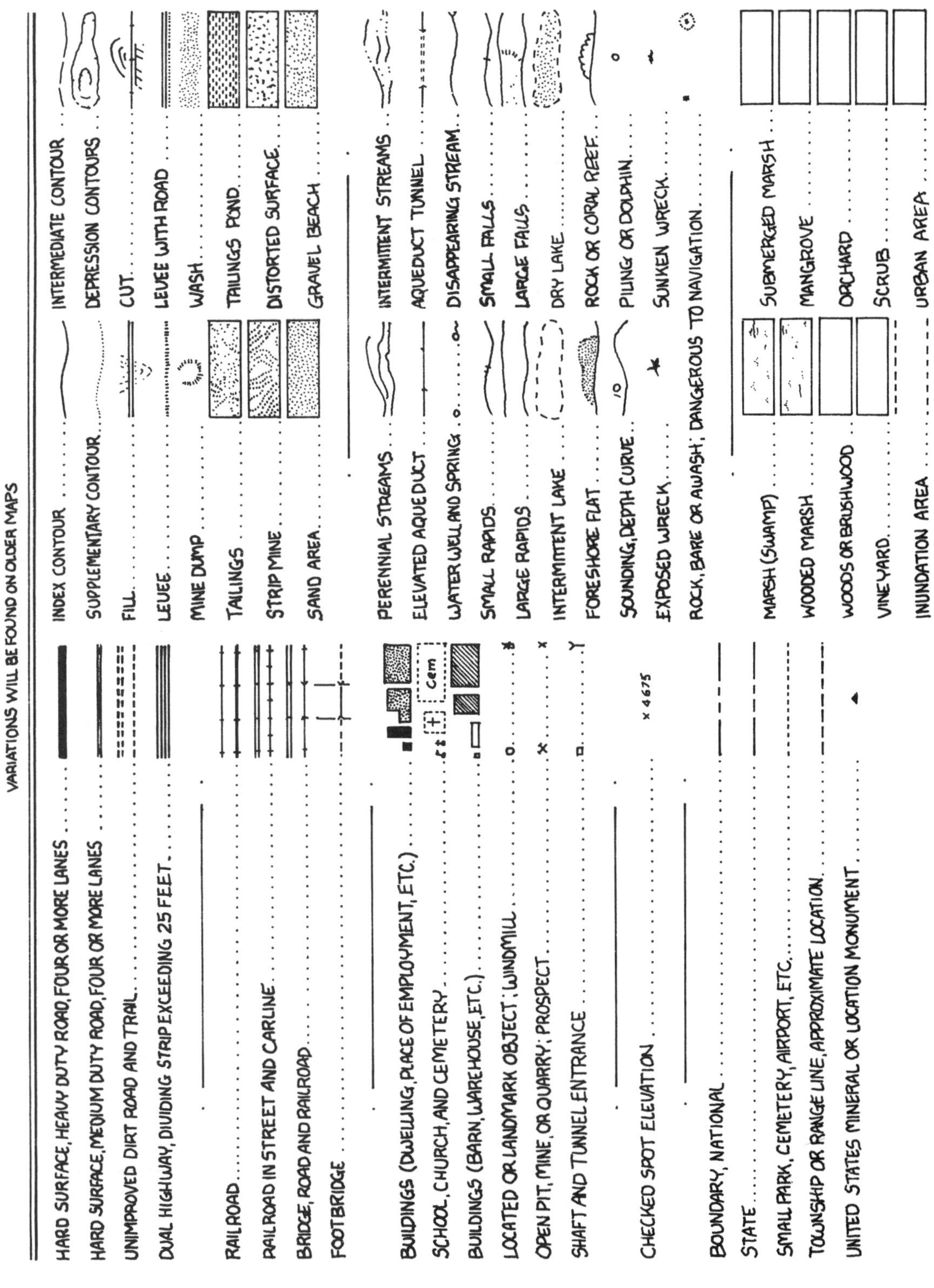

VARIATIONS WILL BE FOUND ON OLDER MAPS

Figure 8.6

HARD SURFACE, HEAVY DUTY ROAD, FOUR OR MORE LANES
HARD SURFACE, MEDIUM DUTY ROAD, FOUR OR MORE LANES
UNIMPROVED DIRT ROAD AND TRAIL
DUAL HIGHWAY, DIVIDING STRIP EXCEEDING 25 FEET
RAILROAD
RAILROAD IN STREET AND CARLINE
BRIDGE, ROAD AND RAILROAD
FOOTBRIDGE
BUILDINGS (DWELLING, PLACE OF EMPLOYMENT, ETC.)
SCHOOL, CHURCH, AND CEMETERY
BUILDINGS (BARN, WAREHOUSE, ETC.)
LOCATED OR LANDMARK OBJECT; WINDMILL
OPEN PIT, MINE OR QUARRY; PROSPECT
SHAFT AND TUNNEL ENTRANCE
CHECKED SPOT ELEVATION   x 4675
BOUNDARY, NATIONAL
STATE
SMALL PARK, CEMETERY, AIRPORT, ETC.
TOWNSHIP OR RANGE LINE, APPROXIMATE LOCATION
UNITED STATES MINERAL OR LOCATION MONUMENT

INDEX CONTOUR
SUPPLEMENTARY CONTOUR
FILL
LEVEE
MINE DUMP
TAILINGS
STRIP MINE
SAND AREA
PERENNIAL STREAMS
ELEVATED AQUEDUCT
WATER WELL AND SPRING
SMALL RAPIDS
LARGE RAPIDS
INTERMITTENT LAKE
FORESHORE FLAT
SOUNDING, DEPTH CURVE
EXPOSED WRECK
ROCK, BARE OR AWASH; DANGEROUS TO NAVIGATION
MARSH (SWAMP)
WOODED MARSH
WOODS OR BRUSHWOOD
VINEYARD
INUNDATION AREA

INTERMEDIATE CONTOUR
DEPRESSION CONTOURS
CUT
LEVEE WITH ROAD
WASH
TAILINGS POND
DISTORTED SURFACE
GRAVEL BEACH
INTERMITTENT STREAMS
AQUEDUCT TUNNEL
DISAPPEARING STREAM
SMALL FALLS
LARGE FALLS
DRY LAKE
ROCK OR CORAL REEF
PILING OR DOLPHIN
SUNKEN WRECK
SUBMERGED MARSH
MANGROVE
ORCHARD
SCRUB
URBAN AREA

Pacing

Measuring your pace plays a critical role in traveling by map and compass. A pace is determined by taking two regular steps and is measured from the heel of the back foot to the toe of the front foot. Your pace may be about 5 feet long (a fairly accurate measure for most adults). Because a pace is two steps, count your paces by counting only each time you put your left (or right) foot down.

The easiest method for determining your pace is to set up a marked distance of 100 feet. From one end, count how many paces it takes you to go 100 feet. Walk the line several times so that your step becomes natural before counting paces or average your paces over several lengths. To determine how many paces are in a mile, take the number of paces you take in 100 feet and multiply by 52.8. Not everyone will end up in exactly the same place, but they should be fairly close to one another.

Helpful Hint

When walking in terrain other than flat terrain, remember that the pacing distance may be a little different going up and down hills. Uphill the pace tends to shorten, and downhill it might lengthen.

Declination

The declination of the map tells you the difference in degrees between true north and magnetic north relative to your location. When using map and compass, you need to adjust for the declination so that you are traveling toward true north versus magnetic north or you may end up a long way from your target. At the bottom of the topo map and to the left of the contour data, you will find an angle. One line points to true north. The other points to the magnetic north. If you are east of a line drawn roughly from Chicago to Florida, the line pointing to magnetic north will be the left of the true north line. If you are west of the Chicago-Florida line, the magnetic line will be on the right of the true north line. This angle shows how far magnetic north is from true north. (Figure 8.7)

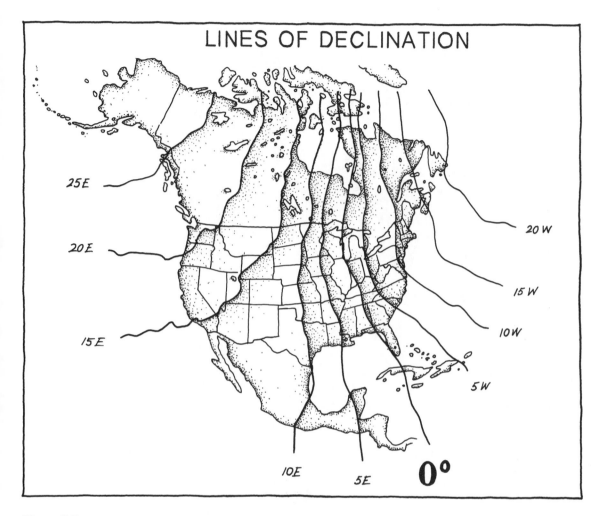

LINES OF DECLINATION

Figure 8.7

Longitude and Latitude

The numbers in the corners of topo maps represent the longitude and latitude. Longitude lines run up and down (vertically), or north and south on the map. Latitude lines run side to side (horizontally) or east and west. These lines are not especially useful for outdoor living skills activities unless you're traveling a great distance or perhaps sailing on the ocean or other large bodies of water.

Many topo maps also feature smaller grids drawn throughout the map and numbers in the margins relating to these lines that indicate townships and ranges. If you do much hiking, you may want to know more about townships and ranges, but it is not necessary for basic map and compass activities.

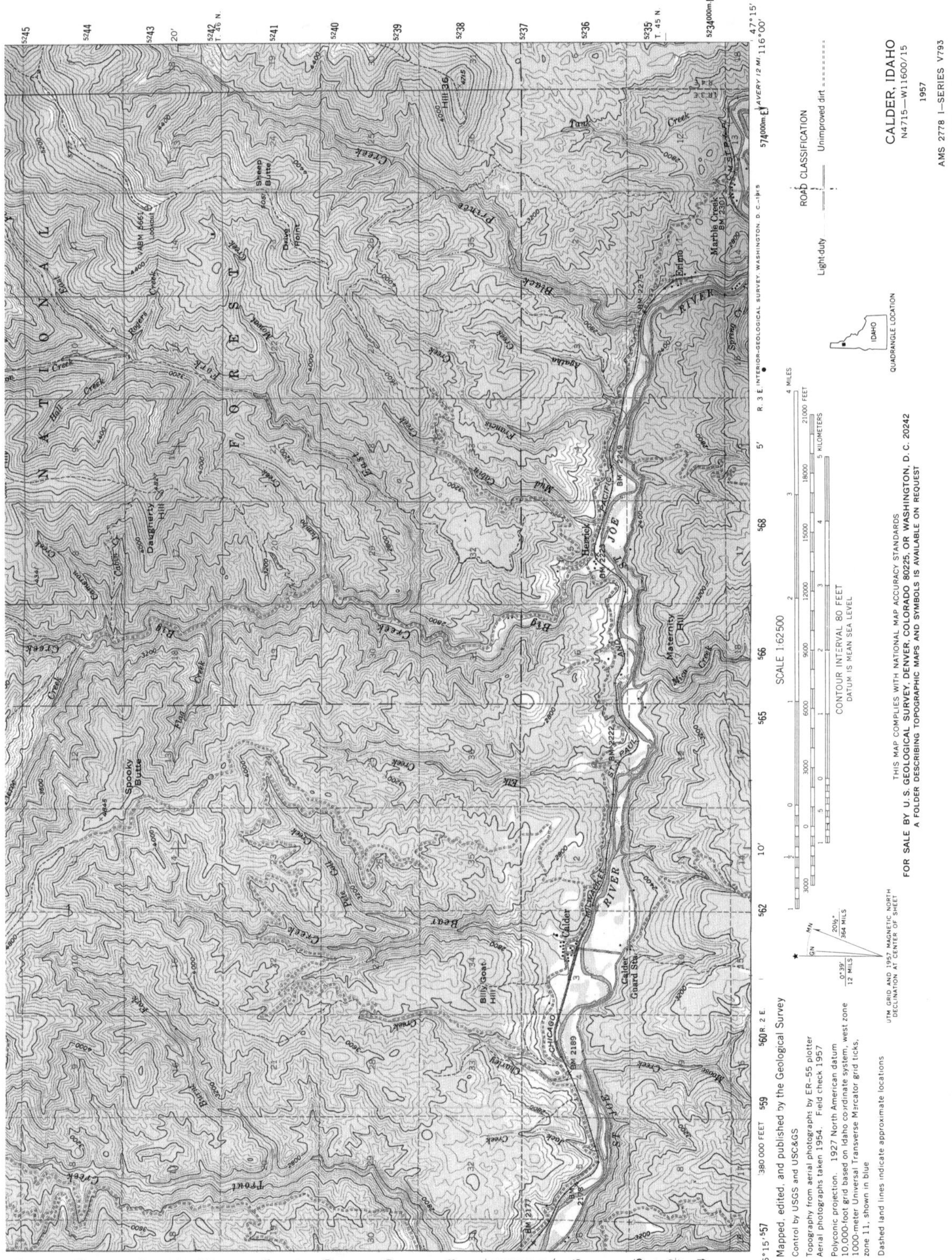
CALDER, IDAHO
N4715—W11600/15
1957
AMS 2778 I—SERIES V793
Mapped, edited, and published by the Geological Survey
Control by USGS and USC&GS
Topography from aerial photographs by ER-55 plotter
Aerial photographs taken 1954. Field check 1957
Polyconic projection. 1927 North American datum
10,000-foot grid based on Idaho coordinate system, west zone
1000-meter Universal Transverse Mercator grid ticks, zone 11, shown in blue
Dashed land lines indicate approximate locations
SCALE 1:62500
CONTOUR INTERVAL 80 FEET
DATUM IS MEAN SEA LEVEL
THIS MAP COMPLIES WITH NATIONAL MAP ACCURACY STANDARDS
FOR SALE BY U. S. GEOLOGICAL SURVEY, DENVER, COLORADO 80225, OR WASHINGTON, D. C. 20242
A FOLDER DESCRIBING TOPOGRAPHIC MAPS AND SYMBOLS IS AVAILABLE ON REQUEST
ROAD CLASSIFICATION
Light-duty
Unimproved dirt
QUADRANGLE LOCATION
IDAHO
UTM GRID AND 1957 MAGNETIC NORTH DECLINATION AT CENTER OF SHEET
NATIONAL FOREST
ST. JOE RIVER
Calder
Herrick
Spooky Butte
Sheep Butte
Daugherty Hill
Maternity Hill
Billy Goat Hill
Calder Guard Sta
(FERNWOOD)

Figure 8.8

Figure 8.8 shows the bottom margin of a topo map of an area in Idaho and a little of the map itself. Locate the name of the map, the location it represents, the date of printing, the scale, and the contour intervals. Describe the area, too. (Is it flat? Hilly? Mountainous? Swampy? Does it have lakes?) What does it look like? What kinds of markers are there? Would it be an easy or difficult hike? What is the line of declination?

Compasses

A compass is a simple but amazing instrument that was developed by the Chinese around 2500 B.C. It works because the earth's magnetic force causes the needle (a piece of magnetized steel) to swing around and point to a particular place in that magnetic field. This place is called magnetic north. If you have a map of the area where you are traveling, you know which part of the map is the north and where you are on the map. If you have a compass, you can find your way to other places on that map.

Selecting a Compass

A compass is an instrument designed to help you travel and show you direction (north, south, east, or west). A variety of compasses are available; however, this exercise requires an orienteering-style compass. Orienteering-style compasses not only show all directions but also allow users to assign a numerical direction or bearing to any direction in the 360° circle that surrounds them. Before you buy a compass let's take a look at the instrument itself.

Most compasses today have plastic base plates on which the compass housing (or bezel), the rotating dial used to determine the bearing, is mounted. The compass housing should be filled with liquid — either water or oil — so that the magnetic needle inside will quickly stop swinging around when the compass is held still; compasses that are not liquid-filled permit the needle to swing for a long time. A liquid-filled compass may be a little more expensive, but it is well worth the extra cost.

The floating needle, housing, and base plate are the mechanical parts of the compass. Each needle has a north end and a south end; the north end may be red or white or have a broader end. Be sure to learn which end of the needle of your compass points north, or you may end up traveling in the opposite direction.

Every compass has lines, numbers, and letters. The direction-of-travel arrow is the most important line; one that is used each time the compass is used. The direction-of-travel arrow, which does not move the way the needle does, is printed on the base plate, outside the compass housing.

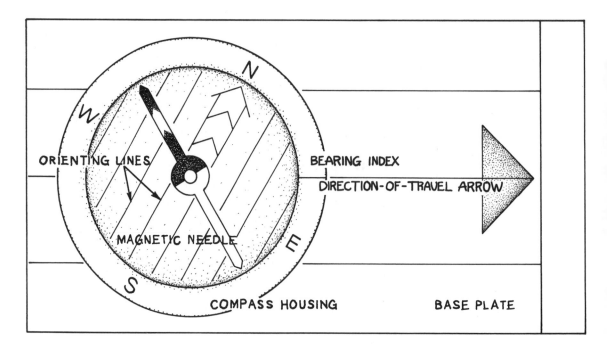

Figure 8.9

The compass housing usually bears letters or numbers indicating north, east, south, and west. Each compass is divided into 360°, or 360 points. North is both 0° and 360°; east is 90°; south is 180°; and west is 270°. The bearings are marked between 2° and 5° intervals. (Figure 8.9)

Fun Fact

The directions north, south, east, and west are also known as cardinal points. The directions northeast, northwest, southeast, and southwest are known as inner cardinal points.

The place where the direction-of-travel arrow and the degrees on the compass housing meet is called the bearing index. This index is where you read bearings (or which way you want to go).

The compass housing also features a set of parallel lines that run north to south. These lines are called the north-south lines or orienting lines. They help to orient the compass to the map.

How to Use a Compass

Hold the compass in the palm of your hand with the direction arrow pointing out between your thumb and index finger. This position keeps the compass squarely in front of you. Turn your body instead of the compass so that the direction of travel is

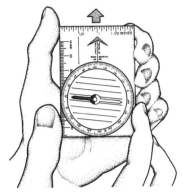

Figure 8.10

always pointing the direction you want to walk. Any time you read a compass, it should remain flat; tilting it or holding it on an angle can give you an inaccurate compass bearing.

The housing will turn easily. Practice coordinating the housing with the direction you want to go. If you want to go 105° as your direction of travel, turn the housing until 105° is at the marker of the direction of travel (Figure 8.10). To line up with that direction, turn your body so that the north end of the compass needle points to the N on the housing, or is lined up with the magnetic north arrow that is printed at the bottom of the compass circle. (Some compasses have them and some don't.) The direction you are facing should be 105°.

Teachable Moment

- First face north. Turn the bezel until north is lined up with the direction-of-travel arrow. Holding the compass correctly, turn your body until the floating needle is aligned with north and the direction-of-travel arrow. You are now facing magnetic north.

- Now face east. Turn the compass housing so that east (or 90°) is lined up with the direction-of-travel arrow. Holding the compass correctly, turn your body until the north end of the needle points to the N, not to the direction-of-travel arrow. You are now facing east, and you have taken a 90° bearing.

- Do the same for south (a 180° bearing) and west (a 270° bearing). Do not worry about the declination.

- Practice the following exercise in an open area or field. Mark the spot where you begin. Travel 5 paces at 90°. Then travel 5 paces at 180°. Next travel 5 paces at 270°. Finally travel 5 paces at 360°. You should end up in the same spot you began. For more of a challenge try the same exercise at 20 paces, 60 paces, and 100 paces.

Helpful Hint

When using a map and compass, stop intermittently (every 100 paces) to site the direction by lining up several points such as trees or other markers. Take additional readings so that you stay in the same heading, especially if you are traveling long distances. Getting off course is easy, particularly if you must walk around trees or lakes or in hilly country.

Adjusting for Declination

To adjust for declination look at the angle at the bottom of the topo map. Your compass needle should point to the angle instead of true north. If you wish to travel true north, set the direction-of-travel arrow on N or 0°. To adjust for a declination of 15° east the compass needs to read 15° (0 + 15). Then follow the compass as previously discussed. If the declination is 15° west, then the direction of travel should read 345° (360 – 15). Remember that a north heading is either 0° or 360°. A trickier compass bearing might be 172°. With a declination of 15° east, set the compass to 187° (172 + 15). Conversely, if the declination is 15° west, the compass heading would be 157° (172 – 15).

Helpful Hints

- Make sure that your belt buckle isn't metal. If it is, the buckle might affect the magnetic end of the needle, making it point to you instead of to north!

- Make sure that the knife in your pocket, the metal snaps on your clothing, the whistle hanging on a lanyard around your neck, or any other nearby metal object does not disturb the magnetic end of the needle.

Geographic North and South

What's the difference between true north and magnetic north? Why does it matter? The geographic north pole and the magnetic north pole are not the same place. The geographic or true north pole is at the geographic top of the earth and is the north pole indicated by maps. Magnetic north is a different place — the place to which all compasses point. Because of mineral deposits in the earth, the earth is like a giant magnet, with one positive, or magnetic pole. Magnetic north is about 1200 to 1400 miles south and west of the true north pole — somewhere north of Hudson Bay and the northern coast of Canada. (Figure 8.11)

Why aren't maps made with magnetic north in mind? Mapmakers start from the equator, which runs true east and west. Because they draw maps from the equator to true (or geographic) north, all map lines run in even lines of longitude and converge at the north pole. If mapmakers made maps go from the equator to magnetic north, the lines would go in different directions. Because of this discrepancy, when you face magnetic north (the north that your compass tells you to face), you are not necessarily facing the same north that your map shows.

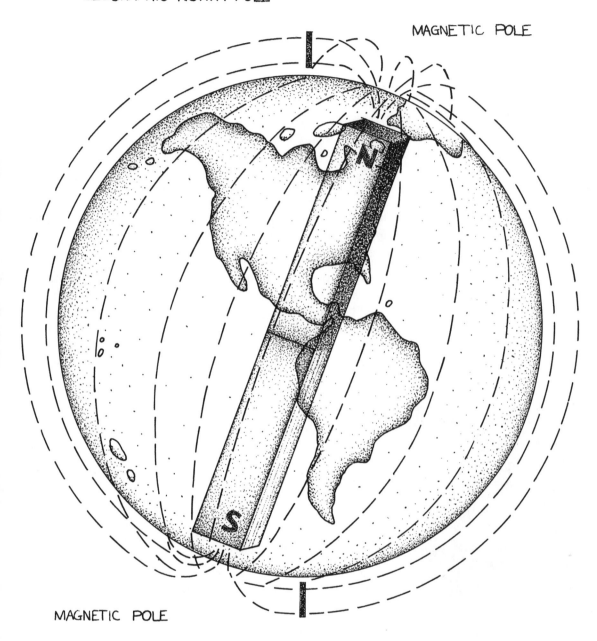

GEOGRAPHIC NORTH POLE

MAGNETIC POLE

MAGNETIC POLE

GEOGRAPHIC SOUTH POLE

Figure 8.11

Orienting Your Map to True North

- Place the map on a flat surface.

- Set the direction of travel arrow on the compass to N (0° or 360°).

- Place the compass parallel to one of the side margins of the map.

- Hold the map and compass steady, and rotate both until the needle comes to stop at the line of declination. (Remember to refer to the bottom of your map for the angle of declination.) The direction of travel is now facing true north. As you move, it is helpful to keep the map oriented to true north.

Your map is now lined up with true north. More expensive compasses have a device for setting the declination angle on the housing, which will help you orient your map. Each time you go to a new area, be sure that you check the declination and reset the marker if necessary.

Locating your starting point on the map before you start the trip is always necessary. Then you can orient the map and read what lies ahead. Plan on a route, estimate your travel time, and anticipate any difficult spots such as steep ravines and streams to cross or places you want to use as rest stops such as springs, meadows, or the shelter of trees.

Using the Map and Compass Together

- Using your compass, orient the map so that it lies true north as explained earlier. (The needle will point to magnetic north.) Keep the map in that position.

- Locate the spot where you are now, and the spot to which you wish to travel.

- Using the side of your compass or something else with a straight edge, make a line between where you are and where you want to go (your direction of travel).

- Lay the compass along the straight line, and rotate the compass until the direction of travel arrow points to the direction you want to go.

- Rotate the housing so that the north end of the needle is pointing to N on the compass.

- You can now read the bearing at the direction-of-travel arrow and begin heading in that direction toward your goal.

- Line up a couple of trees (or other recognizable objects) ahead of you and head for the first one. Then line up a third object with your second object and head for the second object. Keep doing this until you reach your destination.

ACA File Photo

Remember to line your map up with true north every time you stop to take a new bearing. Recheck the bearing using the preceding procedures. In time, you'll be able to line up objects that are farther and farther apart. You'll spend less time taking bearings, and you'll hike more rapidly toward each object and toward your destination. Again, don't forget to stop every now and then to take a bearing so that you don't get too far off track.

It's better to start in a small area such as a local park or county forest to begin your work with map and compass. Do so until you are comfortable with the process and confident that you can get where you are going before heading out into more remote areas.

Reading from Land to Map

ACA File Photo

During your journey, you may want to make a record of your travels so that you can backtrack on your return trip or so that someone else can follow the same trail. To plot your direction of travel on a map as you are hiking, follow these steps:

- Prepare your map for declination.

- Make a dot on the map at your current position.

- Observe the landscape and decide which way you wish to travel. Choose some easily recognizable land formation, bend in the river, or building in the direction that you want to walk. When you are just beginning, choose something that is only 100 yards or less away.

- Read the compass bearing in that direction.

- Place your compass on the oriented map so that its north-south orienting lines are parallel to the true north lines and so that the center of the floating needle is exactly on your current position. The direction-of-travel arrow should be pointing to the land formation on the map that you sighted in the field.

- Draw a line on the map from your current position to the easily recognizable destination, by extending the direction-of-travel arrow with your pencil. Read your bearing on the compass.

- Walk to your chosen destination.

- Observe the landscape again, and choose another easily recognizable destination.

- Repeat these steps the entire time you are walking. You will then be able to retrace your steps to return to your original position by reading from the map to the landscape on the way back or to share your course with others.

When you arrive at each new destination, be sure to turn around for a moment and look back at where you were to recognize landmarks on your return trip.

Compass Courses

To create a compass course for someone else to follow, follow these steps:

ACA File Photo

- Orient your map.

- Locate your starting point on the map.

- Write down a description of the starting point on a piece of paper. "Begin at the park entrance."

- Observe the landscape and choose an easily recognizable land formation, bend in the river, or building as a destination.

- Take a compass bearing in that direction.

- Write down that compass bearing on your paper. "Take a 90° bearing."

- Plot that path from your current position to your first destination on the map.

- Walk to the first destination, counting the paces as you go.

- Write down the number of paces on your piece of paper. "Go 30 paces to the flag pole."

- Observe the landscape and choose another destination.

- Take a compass bearing in that direction.

- Write down that compass bearing on your paper. "Take a 27° bearing."

- Plot that bearing and direction-of-travel line on your map.

- Walk to that destination, counting the paces as you go.

- Write down the number of paces on your paper. "Go 62 paces to the edge of the stream."

- Repeat these steps until your course is as long as you like. If you are in an area where there is no chance of getting lost, you need not plot your directions on the map.

When you finish, your compass course directions might look like this:

Start at the park entrance.
Take a 90° bearing and go 30 paces to the flag pole.
Next, take a 27° bearing and go 62 paces to the edge of the stream.

If you take a creative approach, they might look like this:

To begin your adventure,
at the park entrance you'll need to be,
then follow these directions,
and you'll arrive at the treasure, one, two, three.

Your first set of directions are,
30 paces at 90 degrees,
where you'll the find stars and stripes,
forever blowing in the breeze.

Walk for 62 paces,
from a 27-degree bearing,
find a place where you'd go,
if it's a cooling off you've been craving.

You'll get a blue ribbon,
you found this place in record time,
now it's your turn to make for someone,
another compass course rhyme.

Make your compass course as easy or as difficult as you like, but always make it as much fun as possible. If you are in an area where participants are sure not to get lost, hide the clues along the way so that the participant must find them before continuing. Hide a treasure at the end. Work in groups of two or more. Have each group make a compass course; then have each group follow a course that another group made. Make sure that an adult works with or checks the work of the group making the course so that they don't send another group off on a wild-goose chase.

Global Positioning Systems

The Global Positioning System, or GPS, is an advanced compass that uses a series of 24 or more satellites orbiting the earth to help determine location. Basically GPS is composed of radio transmitters receiving a signal from one or several of the satellites to determine your exact position through the process of triangulation.

The GPS works 24 hours a day, 7 days a week, 365 days a year. It works in good and bad weather and can locate your position even if you are in the middle of the ocean or another body of water with no landmarks. Performance is only limited when the signal from a satellite is blocked from obstacles such as dense forest cover, mountains, or tall buildings. GPS receivers can figure out where you are, where your next campsite is, how far away it is, which direction it is, and what lies between you and your destination. It can also store information from previous excursions so that you can retrace your steps to your favorite hiking trail or campsite. However, GPS cannot work when the satellite is down or when the batteries on your unit wear out. Do not use GPS to replace map and compass skills. It can, however, supplement your map and compass skills. Always, always bring a map and compass with you even if you have a GPS.

For More Information

You can learn more about maps and compasses through a variety of different sources on the Internet and through other resources. A list of suggested references appears in appendix A.

Finding your way by map and compass can be challenging yet rewarding. Not many people have the opportunity to travel in this way without the use of modern technology. Map and compass skills allow you to travel where many people don't travel. You can find your own way through the out-of-doors or retrace historical steps such as the trail of Lewis and Clark. Remember that reading map language and compensating for declination takes practice, but the places you are able to go after you have mastered this skill are innumerable.

Final Thoughts

The outdoors is full of many wonderful places to see. Whether planning a day trip to your local state forest or city park or a week-long excursion to the Boundary waters, preparation is the key to a positive and successful outdoor excursion. Wherever you decide to venture, may you step carefully and travel gently, finding friendship and beauty in the natural world.

"Keep close to nature's heart . . .

and break clear away once in a while,

climb a mountain or spend a week in the woods.

Wash your spirit clean . . .

Go to the mountains and get their glad tidings.

Nature's peace will flow into you as sunshine flows into trees.

The winds will blow their own freshness into you,

and the storms their energy,

while cares will drop off like autumn leaves."

John Muir

Choosing a Place to Go

Each of the following agencies administers federal properties, and each has different policies for their recreational use. You should investigate all categories of recreational land before you select an area in which to practice your outdoor-living skills.

Bureau of Land Management
Office of the Director
U.S. Department of the Interior
Washington, DC 20240
www.blm.gov

Bureau of Land Reclamation
U.S. Department of the Interior
Washington, DC 20240
www.usbr.gov/main/

U.S. Fish and Wildlife Service
Office of the Director
U.S. Department of the Interior
Washington, DC 20240
www.fws.gov

National Park Service
U.S. Department of the Interior
Washington, DC 20240
www.nps.gov

U.S. Forest Service
U.S. Department of Agriculture
Washington, DC 20013
www.fs.fed.us

Check a library for your state-government directory, which contains addresses of park departments, game commissions, tourism bureaus, natural resources departments, conservation departments, and recreation commissions.

Also consider contacting your county and municipal park systems, as well as the youth and adult camps in your area. For a complete list of accredited camps, contact:

American Camping Association
5000 State Road 67 North
Martinsville, IN 46151
(765) 342-8456
or visit www.ACAcamps.org

Exploring Your World Activities

Tuning in the Senses

Concepts

To provide an opportunity for the concentrated use and development of each of the five senses.

To increase participants' awareness of the value of using all five senses as tools for observation.

Time

1 hour and 30 minutes

Season

Any — during dry weather

Location

Anywhere outdoors — preferably a level surface

Number

One to five groups with a maximum of five participants in each group

One leader /station

Materials

Paper (two – five sheets per person)

Pencils (one per person)

Tape (transparent/masking)

Blindfolds (one per person)

Five rings of different sizes

Natural objects: rocks, flowers, pine cones

Optional: table, bench, or flat surface (approximately 3' x 6')

Procedure

• Arrange materials at five stations around tables or in an open area. Each station should be oriented toward a different sense.

Smelling. Ask participants to find and describe five different smells (soil, flowers, fungi, pine cones, etc.). List the descriptions of each smell on a piece of paper. If desired, tape items on a piece of paper.

Seeing. Ask participants to find and describe (color, shape, design, etc.) objects of a specific size. Pass out rings of various sizes so participants can find items that fit through each.

Touching. Ask participants to find and draw or describe objects with different textures (the hairiest leaf, the softest leaf, the smoothest twig, the roughest twig, something cool, something warm, something bumpy, something dry).

Listening. Use natural objects, such as rocks, leaves, and pine cones, to make sounds for participants. Keep the objects from their sight. Have participants close their eyes, or blindfold them, as you make each sound. Then have participants try to describe the sound and the object using analogies and imagination. Write each description on paper. After the activity is completed, discuss the descriptions and/or tape the written descriptions next to each object.

Tasting. Arrange a variety of tasty, natural objects (miner's lettuce, licorice fern, sour grass, pine needles, ginger, etc.) on a table or level surface. Know your area's plants! Blindfold the participants. Pass out pieces of each item to the participants, one at a time, and have them taste the items. Record responses as they taste the items. Encourage analogies and descriptions of the tastes. Tape each item next to its written description.

- Divide participants into groups.

- A leader at each station involves the participants in activities.

- After 15 – 20 minutes, participants rotate to the next station and the leaders involve the next group in the same activity.

Variation

The leader and group rotate together to a new station with a new activity. Continue until all groups have participated in each of the five sense activities.

Safety

- Define boundaries.

- When tasting, allow no swallowing.

- When choosing natural objects for each sense activity, do not disturb the environment.

- Organize — make sure groups stay together.

Adopting a Tree

Concepts

To see things with more than just our eyes.

Time

45 minutes

Season

Any

Location

A natural wooded area

Number

12 participants maximum

Materials

Blindfolds (one per person)

40' rope

Procedure

• Blindfold participants to heighten the other senses.

• Evenly space participants along the rope and lead them into an area with a lot of trees. As you guide the group along by the rope, "drop off" one participant at a time at different trees. Have participants remain blindfolded.

• Ask participants to explore their tree friend. Hug it. Rub their cheeks against it. Listen to it or try to hear the life inside it. Smell it. Explore its trunk with their fingers, nose, or skin. Check out its base. Feel the patterns on the trunk. Is anything living on it? How big is it? Instruct participants to be silent and stay with their tree until a leader comes back for them.

• Round up all the participants on the rope, lead them back to the starting point, and ask them to take off their blindfolds.

• Ask participants to go and find their friendly tree, using all of their senses. After the participants find their trees, ask them to take a moment and to see how beautiful the tree is.

• Discuss the activity: What feelings were experienced? What different methods were used to identify trees? Have participants describe what they felt, smelled, heard, and tasted.

Variations

• Blindfold participants after a short spin to erase their sense of direction. Then guide each participant to a tree.

- When it is time to return to the starting point, ask participants to listen to your voice and turn to face the direction it is coming from. Continue talking and ask them to walk from their trees to you, taking off the blindfolds only when they reach you. When all participants have found their way back by listening to your voice, ask each participant to remove his or her blindfold and to find his or her tree.

Safety

- Keep everyone in sight.

- Don't allow anyone to wonder off blindfolded.

- Walk slowly and carefully when leading the blindfolded group on the rope.

- Before leaving any participant alone, make sure he or she is touching the tree you want him or her to explore.

Once You've Seen One, You've Seen 'Em All. Haven't You?

Concepts

To have participants understand the strength of the sense of touch.

To have participants understand that no two things are identical.

Time

15 – 20 minutes

Season

Any

Location

Any — outdoors preferable

Number

Any

Materials

One small rock per person (leaves or twigs may be used depending on the ability of group)

Blindfolds (one per person; optional)

Procedure

- Have participants stand or sit in a circle, blindfolded or with their hands behind their backs.

- Give one rock to each person, and tell everyone to get to know his or her rock through touch only. If participants are not blindfolded, make sure that they keep their hands behind their backs.

- Let participants feel, scratch, pat their rocks. Let them find grooves, edges, and any other qualities that their rock may have.

- Collect the rocks and redistribute them in a different order. Instruct participants to feel the new rock behind their back to see if it is theirs.

- Have participants pass the rock on to the next person if the rock they hold is not their original rock. Have them continue to pass the rocks until they find their own. Try to get each rock back to its original owner.

- Let participants keep their rocks or ask them to find a home in the woods for it when the activity is over.

Variation

To make it easier, let participants look at their rock for one minute before collecting and redistributing the rocks.

Safety

No specific safety guidelines for this activity

My Leaf

Concepts

To develop participants' sense of touch to help them know natural objects fully.

Time

20 minutes

Season

Spring, summer, fall

Location

Woods or meadow

Number

5 to 15 participants

Materials

One leaf per person

Procedure

- Instruct participants to close their eyes and leave them closed until you say they can open them.

- Give each participant a leaf and tell him or her to get to know the leaf using hands only.

- Let them feel the leaves for five minutes.

- Gather the leaves and put them in a pile.

- Instruct participants to open their eyes and to find their leaves in the pile.

- Discuss the different details that could be felt with hands, but might be missed with the eyes.

Safety

No specific safety guidelines for this activity

Scavenger Hunt

Concepts

To develop participants' awareness of their sense of observation and knowledge of their natural environment.

To provide a nature exploration experience.

To use nature for recreation.

To operate in a group with good sportsmanship.

Time

1 ½ to 2 hours

Season

Any — preferably a dry season

Location

Any outdoor site

Number

Maximum of five groups with three or four people in each

Materials

A container (bag or sack)

A list of natural objects

Pencil (one per group)

Paper (one per group)

Procedure

• Divide participants into groups (informally), and give each group a container.

• Set a time limit (1 ½ hour) and boundaries for exploration.

• Hand out a list of items to be found and collected.

Suggested List

the hairiest leaf

the softest leaf

the smoothest twig

the roughest twig

something cool

something warm

something bumpy

something dry

something with grooves

something triangular

something sweet

something fuzzy

something circular

something bright

something symmetrical

• Instruct groups to stay within the boundary and find as many of the items on their list as possible without disturbing the environment.

• Call the groups back together at a designated place and share the items found.

• Let participants use these items for a craft project.

• Have participants discuss the objects that weren't brought back to the group. How would bringing them back have disturbed the natural environment?

Safety

- Define boundaries for the scavenger hunt.

- Prevent disturbance of the natural environment by instructing participants not to destroy an object's habitat area.

- Instruct participants to draw or describe an object and its location if the object cannot be brought back without disturbing anything.

Outer Space Visitor

Concepts

To increase participants' observation skills, use of descriptive language, and analogies.

Time

10 – 15 minutes

Season

Any

Location

Any (good fill-in activity while waiting)

Number

Any

Materials

None

Procedure

- Have participants pretend they have just arrived by rocketship at another planet. They are standing on a planet that is completely foreign to them and are looking at things for the first time!

- Ask each participant to select an object (a tree, rock, flower, cloud) and describe it without using words that would ordinarily apply. Words such as trunk, bark, leaves, twigs, buds, petal, blossom may not be used.

- Have the group guess what object is being described. The participant who first recognizes the object takes the next turn.

Safety

No specific safety guidelines for this activity

What Is It?

Concepts

To have participants describe an object with clues.

To have participants work as a unit.

To have participants really think about the features of an object.

Time

30 minutes

Season

Any

Location

Outdoors

Number

Three groups of five or six members

One leader for each group

Materials

Pencil and paper

Procedure

- Divide the group into three smaller groups.

- Instruct each group to gather four or five natural objects (leaves, flowers, seeds, insects, etc.) without destroying the environment.

- After the objects are gathered, discuss each object within the smaller groups without letting the other groups see.

- After all groups have discussed their objects, start the contest.

- Have group A offer two clues about an object they have and let groups B and C try to guess the object. If the other groups can't guess, have group A offer one more clue, and again let groups B and C guess. Continue until group A has offered six clues. If groups B and C are still unable to guess, then have group A tell them and receive a point.

- Have group B offer two clues, and let groups A and C guess.

- Repeat this process if groups A and C are unable to guess the object. Continue the game until each of the objects has been presented.

- At the conclusion of the game, have each group draw their objects from memory.

- Discuss why each object was found, where it was found, and if there is any interrelationship between the objects.

Safety

No specific safety guidelines for this activity

Back-to-Back Observation

Concepts

To develop participants' ability to describe precisely.

To develop participants' use of analogies in describing things.

Time

30 minutes

Season

Any

Location

Any

Number

Two groups of two to ten people

Materials

Two sets of two bags of identical natural materials with five items per bag (pine cones, leaves, rocks, twigs, acorns, etc.)

Procedure

- Divide the group in two smaller groups. Have each group stand or sit with their backs to the other group. Give each group a bag of items to spread out in front of them.

- Instruct one group to select an item from the bag, describing it so that the other group can pick the same item out of its bag.

- Have group 1 explain exactly how they are placing the item on the ground in front of them. Group 2 must place the identical item in an identical position in front of them.

- Have group 1 select another item, describe it to group 2, and explain how to place it in relation to the previous item. Continue until both groups have placed all their objects.

- Compare to see if group 2's objects are in the same relative position as group 1's objects.

- Trade roles and use different objects.

Rules for Description

- Groups may not use words to describe the object's name, color, or material.

- They may use words to describe the object's size, shape, feel, or odor.

Variation

This activity may also be done with different items of varying descriptive difficulty such as five different leaves, all kinds of rocks, or flowers of different species.

Safety

No specific safety guidelines for this activity

Leaf Rubbings

Concepts

To have participants make leaf rubbings.

To have participants understand differences in leaf types.

Time

20 minutes to 1 hour

Season

Late spring through early fall

Location

Any area with different types of plants

Number

Any

Materials

Thin paper

A flat surface

Leaves (to be collected by participants)

Natural rubbing materials (charcoal, fleshy leaves, bark, soil, etc.)

Procedure

- Explain that there are many kinds of plants with leaves of varied shapes and sizes.

- Instruct participants to collect different leaves and natural drawing materials.

- Have participants place a leaf vein-side up on a flat surface and then place a sheet of paper over the leaf, holding the leaf and the paper firmly in place.

- With the other hand, have the participants rub the charcoal or other rubbing material in parallel strokes over the leaf. The outline and venation of the leaf will appear on the paper.

- Have participants make a booklet of rubbings.

Safety

Avoid poisonous plants. Make sure participants know what the local poisonous plants look like.

Diving Bell

Concepts

To allow participants to explore life in the water and watch animals being attracted to light.

Time

30 minutes in late evening or at night

Season

Late spring through early fall, depending on the climate (in some places this activity could be used anytime)

Location

Pond, lake, or any still or slow moving body of water that has a dock or a pier

Number

Any

Materials

Large jar with a tight-fitting lid (a mayonnaise jar, for instance)

Weight (rock)

Flashlight

Rope

Procedure

- Have participants place the illuminated flashlight and a weight in the jar, seal the jar tightly, and tie the rope around the jar so that one long end of the rope is free.

- Lower the diving bell into the water.

- Watch animals being attracted to the light source.

- Observe and discuss animal life.

Safety

No specific safety guidelines for this activity

Cinquain Poetry

Concepts

To introduce participants to an easy, enjoyable writing experience utilizing the outdoors.

Time

30 minutes

Season

Any

Location

Any

Number

Any

Materials

Pencil and paper

Procedure

- Have participants observe features in the outdoors.

- Compose a cinquain as a group.

- Let individuals compose a cinquain.

Cinquain Form

raccoon	1 word naming subject
playful, funny	2 describing words
creeps slowly onward	3 words of action
silently stalks the grasshopper	4 words of activity, effect
hunter	1-word synonym for the subject, or a summary

Have participants share their poems or display them on a bulletin board.

Safety

No specific safety guidelines for this activity

Haiku Poetry

Concepts

To introduce participants to an easy, enjoyable writing experience about the outdoors.

To use syllables to write a poem about nature.

Time

30 minutes or more

Season

Any

Location

Any

Number

Any

Materials

Pencils

Paper

Paint, crayons, pastels, etc.

Procedure

Explain to participants that the haiku is a form of Japanese poetry about nature, that it need not rhyme, and that it is based on numbers of syllables in each of three lines.

Haiku Form

Winter	title
The star studded tree	5 syllables
Shivers in the pale moonlight	7 syllables
The wind rushes by	5 syllables

• Let individuals compose a haiku.

• After writing, let participants illustrate the poems.

Safety

No specific safety guidelines for this activity

Art Form Hunt

Concepts

To expose participants to art forms in nature.

To have participants become aware of patterns, shapes, lines, textures, and colors.

To relate natural forms to man-made forms.

To look for similarity and variety.

Time

30 minutes to 1 hour

Season

Any

Location

Any outdoor location

Number

Groups of four to five participants

A leader in each group

Materials

Pencils and notebooks

List of art forms to look for

Procedure

- Have groups of four to five participants plus a leader explore patterns, art forms, and colors in a natural environment, recording what and where they are found.

- Find examples of: five shapes, ten shades of color, three horizontal lines, four vertical lines, four diagonal lines, five patterns (repetitions), and five textures.

- Discuss findings.

Safety

No specific safety guidelines for this activity

Peanut Patch

Concepts

To have participants learn that living things adjust and change, or adapt, to cope with their environment, even in one lifetime.

To introduce the D.A.M. Law — Die, Adapt, or Move.

Time

20 minutes

Season

Any

Location

Any

Number

8 to 12 participants

Materials

Large bag of peanuts in the shell

Empty bag for storage of empty shells

Masking tape

Scissors

Procedure

- Divide group into two smaller groups.

- Have one of the groups watch carefully while the other group stands or sits in a line while you throw some peanuts to them and ask them to crack and eat the peanuts.

- Tape the thumbs of the participants in the second group to their palms, and have them stand or sit in a line.

- Have the first group watch as you throw some peanuts to the second group. Ask the second group to crack and eat the peanuts.

- Discuss how easy it was to eat the peanuts. If the people in the second group were able to eat the peanuts, even without their thumbs, they solved the problem. The way they solved the problem is an example of adaptation. Discuss the importance of an opposable thumb. Could they have adapted in any other way? Consider whether they could have found some other food that didn't need to be cracked open. Discuss plants and animals that have adapted. (Adaptation is a change of function in one lifetime while evolution is the process by which adaptation is passed on to following generations.)

- Have the participants clean up the peanut shells.

Safety

No specific safety guidelines for this activity

Circle of Life (Building Images)

Concepts

To have participants understand that all plants, animals, and substances in nature are interrelated with others in some way (e.g., some things feed on others, some are eaten by others, some protect others, some decompose others).

To have participants understand that humans are ultimately the chief predators in the natural environment.

To have participants understand that "there is no free lunch" means that nothing in nature gets something without a consequence.

To have participants understand that "everything is going somewhere" means that the natural environment is always changing; nothing remains in the same state over a long period of time.

Time

20 – 30 minutes

Season

Any

Location

Any — around a table, campfire, or outside in a circle

Number

12 participants maximum

Materials

Variety of objects from nature (pine cone, leaf, insect, etc.)

Procedure

- Have your group sit in a circle.

- Pick up an object from nature, and show it to the group.

- Have one person start the game by taking the object and naming a plant, animal, or other object in nature that feeds on, is eaten by, protects, is protected by, or decomposes the object you picked up.

- Have the participant pass the object to the next person. That person then names something else that would be associated with the object in any of these ways.

- Failure to give an answer within a given time earns a participant the first letter of the word "DEAD." If a person receives all of the letters from the word "DEAD," he or she is out of the game. Any answer may be challenged by any other person in the game. A challenge can be accepted or denied by the group. If the group accepts the challenge, the person who was challenged receives a letter.

Variation

Add other rules to increase the difficulty of the game such as not allowing participants to repeat any previously mentioned object.

Safety

- Do not pass objects that are pointed or can be harmful.

- Do not use fragile or delicate objects such as bird eggs — help protect nature.

Forest Community

Concepts

To help participants understand that a city community and a natural community (forest, meadow, marsh, etc.) have similar items that help the community thrive.

To help participants understand that different functions allow all different kinds of communities to coexist and function. Each item is related to another — each has a function and is dependent on another for survival.

To help participants understand that plants and animals need one another to live together in communities, similar to the way humans use and live with each other and natural resources.

Time

1 hour

Season

Any

Location

Outdoors in a natural area

Number

8 to 10 participants

Materials

Pencil and paper

Procedure

- Have the group list all the parts that a town or city has. Relate this to the participants' hometown or neighborhood.

  Suggestions for the List

  inhabitants

  plumbing

  communications system

  factories

  stores

  cafeterias

  apartments

  garbage collectors

  energy sources

  traffic

  streets

  transportation

- Divide the group into smaller groups.

- Send each group out to locate items in nature that are similar to those on the list.

- Bring the group members back together to share their findings.

- Discuss how things in nature depend on one another, work together, and live interdependently. Discuss what things participants found in nature that play roles that are similar to those found in a city.

Safety

- Set boundaries for exploration.

- Set a time limit for returning to the group.

- Do not collect the items; simply look and make note of things.

What Eats?

Concepts

To illustrate to participants the concept of the food chain.

Time

20 – 30 minutes

Location

A room with a blackboard

Number

Any

Materials

Blackboard

1 piece of chalk per team

Procedure

- Divide the group into teams, with no more than ten participants on a team. On the blackboard, write a column of numbers, one to ten, for each team. Give each team a piece of chalk.

- Have each team stand away from its column of numbers.

- At a signal, direct the first person on each team to dash to his or her team's column of numbers and write the name of a plant or an animal next to the first number and then dash back and give the chalk to the second person on the team.

- The second person in line should dash to the blackboard, write the name of something that eats what was written in the number one spot, and return the chalk to the next person in line.

- The third person in line writes on the blackboard the name of something that eats what was written in the number two spot and returns the chalk to the next person in line.

- Continue playing the game until one team has reached number ten. If a player writes down an incorrect name, it may be erased, but only by the very next player, who loses his or her turn to write a name. This means that a turn is lost each time a team makes an error.

- To determine the winning team, allow one point for each correct link in the chain represented in the column. If an item is incorrect, a point is lost, but the scoring continues from that point.

• The first time a group plays this game, scores probably will be low. There may also be considerable discussion about right and wrong answers. Using books to answer questions and settle arguments is one way to learn about food chains. Each time the game is played, participants will know more and more about what eats what, the competition will be more exciting, and the game more fun.

Variation

Once a group has developed some skill at playing, try limiting the habitat to that of the forest, a brook, a marsh, a pond, the ocean, or some particular community. Perhaps you can even limit the season of the year or the time of day.

Safety

No specific safety guidelines for this activity

Putting It on Your Plate

Recipes

There are literally hundreds and probably thousands of recipes you can use outdoors. The ones presented here represent only a small portion of the easy ones. They are presented to give you a variety of things you can prepare with simple ingredients, a few utensils, and a stove or small fire. Remember open fires should only be used in a designated fire ring unless it is an emergency situation. Some of the items will require cooking at home; some use perishable foods and are intended for base camp cooking; others are for meals on the extended trip.

For trips away from base camp, plan simple menus with little cooking and no perishable foods. At base camp, try something more elaborate and time-consuming. Outdoor cooking can be fun as long as you are prepared.

In all cases, practice before deciding which will be part of your permanent collection. Then look for more recipes until you have found a wide selection of delicious items.

Beverages

Cocoa

Serves: 1 person

Method: kettle

Approximate time: 10 minutes

> 1 teaspoon cocoa
>
> 2 teaspoons sugar
>
> 4 tablespoons milk powder
>
> 1 cup water
>
> salt

Mix cocoa and sugar with water in a small pan and bring to a boil. Add milk powder and stir thoroughly. Reduce heat to a simmer and continue stirring to prevent any scum from forming. Serve when all ingredients are incorporated.

Spiced Hot Tea

Serves: 10 people

Method: kettle

Approximate time: 10 minutes

    2 cups orange-flavored instant breakfast drink

    3/4 teaspoon cinnamon

    2 cups sugar (try using 1 cup)

    1 ½ cups instant tea

    1/4 teaspoon nutmeg

    1 4-oz. package instant lemonade

In base camp or at home, mix all ingredients together. Store in a tightly sealed can. To make 1 cup of spiced tea, add 1 cup boiling water to 2 teaspoons mix.

Cereals

Crunch Dry Cereal

Serves: 8 to 10 people

Method: oven

Approximate time: 40 minutes

    3 cups rolled oats

    1 cup wheat germ

    1 cup sesame seeds or sunflower seeds

    1 cup shredded, unsweetened coconut

    1/3 cup oil

    3/4 cup honey

    1 teaspoon vanilla

    dash of salt

In base camp or at home, mix all ingredients together. Spread mixture ½-inch deep on cookie pan and bake at 350°F until golden brown. Stir occasionally because the sides will brown first. Let cool. Good for breakfast with milk, or for trail lunch.

Granola

Serves: makes 3 pounds

Method: oven

Approximate time: 40 minutes

  4 cups rolled oats

  1 cup wheat germ

  1 cup sunflower seeds

  3/4 cup shredded coconut

  1/2 cup sesame seeds

  1 cup chopped nuts

  1/2 cup oil

  3/4 cup honey

  1 ½ teaspoons vanilla

  1 to 2 cups raisins

In base camp or at home, mix the dry ingredients in a large bowl. Heat oil, honey, and vanilla until combined. Pour mixture over dry ingredients and mix well. Spread on greased cookie sheet. Bake at 350°F for 20 to 30 minutes or until lightly browned. Stir frequently. Add raisins when cool. Good with milk for trail lunch or for snack.

Homemade Cereal

Serves: 10 to 12 people

Method: oven

Approximate time: 45 minutes

  2 cups rolled oats

  1 cup wheat germ

  2 ½ teaspoons sesame seeds

  1 cup shredded coconut

  1/2 cup nuts

  3/4 cup raisins

  1/2 cup chopped dates

  1/4 teaspoon cinnamon

1/4 teaspoon allspice

1/2 teaspoon salt

3/4 cup molasses

1/3 cup salad oil

1/2 teaspoon vanilla

Preheat oven to 300°F. Mix dry ingredients in a large bowl. Add molasses, oil, and vanilla, and mix. Spread on baking sheets and heat for 30 minutes, stirring often. Cool. Store in airtight container. Serve with milk.

Mountain Cereal

Serves: 24 people

Method: oven

Approximate time: 30 minutes

In a large bowl, mix together:

4 ½ cups rolled oats

1 ½ cups pumpkin seeds, chopped

2 cups sunflower seeds

1 cup shredded coconut

1/4 cup sesame seeds, ground in blender

In a separate bowl, blend together:

1/2 cup warm water

3/4 cup honey

1/4 cup oil

1 teaspoon salt

Mix all ingredients well and bake at 275°F, stirring often, until golden brown (about 10 minutes). Add:

2 cups dried currants or raisins

1/2 cup dried banana flakes

Stir often as mixture cools. Store in sealed bag in refrigerator.

Note: Cereals can be made in advance at home and stored in plastic bags; however, homemade cereals do not have any preservatives in them and may not last as long as a store-bought brand.

Soups

Curried Vegetable Soup

Serves: 4 people

Method: kettle

Approximate time: 25 minutes

At home: Bag together 1 package dried onion soup mix; 1/4 cup each dried tomatoes, carrots, celery, and onion; 2 beef bouillon cubes; 1/2 teaspoon curry powder, and salt and pepper to taste.

In camp: Bring 5 ½ cups of water to a boil.

Simmer 15 minutes.

Serve.

Vigorous Veggie Soup

Serves: 4 people

Method: kettle

Approximate time: 25 minutes

At home: Bag together 1/2 cup each dried potatoes and carrots, 1/4 cup each dried celery and onions, 2 chicken bouillon cubes, these seasonings to taste: marjoram, salt and pepper, paprika, caraway seed, dill seed.

In camp: Bring 5 ½ cups of water to a boil.

Add dry ingredients plus 1/2 cup margarine and 1/4 cup dry milk.

Simmer 15 minutes.

Cheese Soup

Serves: 4 people

Method: kettle

Approximate time: 30 minutes

At home: Bag together 1/4 cup each dried carrots, celery, peppers, and onion and 2 bouillon cubes. In a second bag put 1 cup sunflower seed kernels and 1/4 cup dry milk.

In camp: Bring 5 ½ cups of water to a boil.

Add dry ingredients from the first bag.

Simmer contents for 15 minutes.

Add second bag plus 1/4 cup margarine and 1 ½ cup grated cheese.

Heat until cheese is melted.

Snacks

GORP (the famous trail snack)

Serves: 10 to 12 people on trail

Method: noncooking

Approximate time: 15 minutes

GORP actually stands for Good Ole Raisins and Peanuts, but any combination of mixed nuts, sunflower seeds, M&Ms, raisins, shredded coconut, and butterscotch drops is good. This is a very handy, high-energy trail snack. Mix equal portions of all ingredients.

Fruit Balls

Serves: 10 to 12 people

Method: noncooking

Approximate time: 15 minutes

Grind together dried figs and raisins, mix in some peanut butter and flaked coconut. Roll into balls. Roll in chopped nuts if desired.

Variations

In amounts to suit your taste, grind together dried apricots, raisins, and dates. Shape into balls and roll in sesame seeds or chopped nuts.

Roasted Pumpkin and Sunflower Seeds

Serves: 10 to 12 people

Method: oven

Approximate time: 10 – 15 minutes

Roast raw seeds in butter on a cookie sheet in the oven, over low heat until pumpkin seeds are slightly puffy. Season with salt, soy sauce, chili powder, etc. Stir well.

One-Pot Dishes

American Chop Suey

Serves: 8 people

Method: kettle

Approximate time: 30 minutes

> 2 teaspoons cooking oil
>
> 3 – 4 onions (small), peeled and diced
>
> green pepper (if desired), cut small
>
> 1 – 1 ½ lbs. ground beef
>
> 2 16-oz. cans spaghetti with tomato sauce
>
> salt and pepper

Fry onions and pepper in oil until brown. Pour off excess oil in a container to pack out. Add ground beef and cook until well done, but not crisply brown. Add spaghetti and heat well. Season to taste. Serve hot.

Variations

Eliminate the ground beef and serve as a veggie dish.

Instead of canned spaghetti, use 1 package macaroni and 1 16-oz. can concentrated tomato soup. Cook macaroni in boiling water. (Takes an extra kettle.) Use a little sausage meat with the ground beef; add some cooked celery or peas.

Scrambled Potatoes

Serves: 8 people

Method: skillet

Approximate time: 20 minutes

> 8 medium-sized, cold, boiled potatoes, diced
>
> 2 small onions, peeled and diced
>
> 4 pieces bacon, chopped, or small amount bacon fat
>
> 8 eggs
>
> salt and pepper

Fry onions with bacon pieces or in bacon fat until light brown. Add potatoes, and fry until brown and crisp. Break eggs into mixture, stirring while it cooks; cook until eggs are set. Season well. Serve hot.

Variation

Add a little cheese or tomato ketchup or both, if desired.

Chili Con Carne

Serves: 8 people

Method: kettle

Approximate time: 30 minutes

> 4 tablespoons cooking oil
>
> 8 tablespoons (about) chopped onion
>
> 1 ½ to 2 lbs. ground beef or leftover meat
>
> 2 qts. canned tomatoes
>
> 2 cans kidney beans
>
> chili powder
>
> salt
>
> flour
>
> 2 tablespoons Worcestershire sauce

Fry onion in cooking oil until light brown. Add meat and cook until done. Add tomatoes and beans and cook together. Season with a little chili powder and salt. Let it all simmer. Thicken with a little flour if needed. Add Worcestershire sauce, if more seasoning is needed.

Campfire Stew

Serves: 8 people

Method: kettle

Approximate time: 30 minutes

> 1 ½ to 2 lbs. ground beef
>
> salt and pepper
>
> 3 teaspoons cooking oil or shortening
>
> 1 large onion, peeled and diced
>
> 2 cans concentrated vegetable soup
>
> water

Make little balls of hamburger, adding salt and pepper. Fry in cooking oil with onion in frying pan, or in bottom of kettle, until onion is light brown and meatballs are well browned all over. Pour off excess grease. Add vegetable soup and enough water to prevent sticking. Cover and cook slowly until meatballs are cooked thoroughly (the longer, the better).

Master Plan One-Pot Meals

Serves: 10 people

Method: Dutch oven or kettle

Approximate time: 30 minutes

Master plan ingredients:

> 2 lbs. hamburger
>
> 2 tablespoons dehydrated onions or finely chopped onion
>
> 2 cans tomato soup
>
> 2 teaspoons dehydrated sweet peppers or 1/2 fresh pepper — chopped
>
> salt and pepper

To prepare master pot, brown hamburger with onions and pepper. Drain grease. Add soup, season, and add ingredients to make any of the following variations.

Master Plan Variation One — Macaroni Beef

> 1 12-oz. package macaroni

Boil macaroni according to instructions on package. Drain macaroni and add to master pot. Serve.

Master Plan Variation Two — Chili

> 3 no. 2 cans red kidney beans
>
> 2 no. 2 cans tomatoes (broken)
>
> chili powder to taste

Add beans, tomatoes, and chili powder to master pot. Simmer 10 minutes and serve.

Master Plan Variation Three — Sloppy Joes

> 10 hamburger buns

Cook master pot to desired consistency and serve on buns.

Master Plan Variation Four — Hunter's Stew

2 no. 2 cans mixed vegetables

3 no. 2 cans of other vegetables such as potatoes, corn, green beans and tomatoes

Add vegetables to master pot. Simmer 10 minutes and serve.

Master Plan Variation Five — Spanish Rice

1 small package instant rice

3 cups water

Add water to master pot and bring to boil. Add rice and remove from heat. Cover with lid and let stand for 5 minutes. Serve.

Master Plan Variation Six — Hungarian Hot Pot

3 no. 2 cans pork and beans

Add pork and beans to master pot. Simmer 10 minutes and serve.

Master Plan Variation Seven — Mexican Delight

1 no. 2 can Mexicorn

1 small jar pitted black olives (optional)

1 small box cornbread mix, plus ingredients noted on package

1 cup water

Add water to master pot and bring to boil. Mix cornbread mix, Mexicorn, and olives. Drop by spoonfuls into master pot. Cover. Do not peek! Cook 15 minutes.

Master Plan Variation Eight — Tacos

2 packets of taco seasoning

onion

lettuce

cheese

tomatoes

taco sauce

taco shells or tortillas

Add taco seasoning to the master pot. Dice the tomatoes and onions. Shred the lettuce and the cheese. Create tacos using the beef mixture and diced and shredded ingredients in a taco shell or tortilla.

One-Pot Spaghetti

Serves: 10 people

Method: Dutch oven or kettle

Approximate time: 45 minutes

> 2 medium onions, chopped
>
> 2 lbs. hamburger
>
> 2 no. 2 cans tomatoes (broken up)
>
> 2 cups water
>
> garlic powder
>
> 16 oz. spaghetti broken in small pieces
>
> 2 tablespoons oregano (optional)

Brown hamburger with onions until tender. Pour off grease. Add remaining ingredients. Bring to boil for 1 minute. Simmer 25 more minutes covered, stirring occasionally. Serve.

Cascade Stew

Serves: 4 people

Method: kettle

Approximate time: 35 minutes

Cook in 4 cups water for 10 minutes:

> 1/3 cup instant potatoes
>
> 1/4 cup dried tomato and carrot chunks
>
> 1 Tablespoon dried onion
>
> 1 Tablespoon dried celery
>
> 2 beef bouillon cubes

Stir in 1/3 cup instant potatoes. When thickened, add 1 can roast beef chunks (or leftover beef from home). Heat through and serve.

Rice and Vegetable Dinner Mix

Serves: 4 to 6 people

Method: kettle

Approximate time: 30 minutes

Bring to a boil in 3 cups water:

>   1/2 cup dried onion
>
>   1/2 cup dried carrots
>
>   1/4 cup dried parsley
>
>   salt and pepper to taste
>
>   3 bouillon cubes

Add 1 ¼ cups quick brown rice and simmer until tender. Top with margarine or cheese. Serve this elegant camp dish for a special trip.

Super-Scramble

Serves: dependent on amount of ingredients added

Method: skillet

Approximate time: 30 minutes

Amount of ingredients should be determined by group size.

>   dried potato shreds
>
>   crumbled meat or bacon bar
>
>   water
>
>   dried onion
>
>   dried parsley
>
>   dried pepper flakes
>
>   cheese, cubed

Soak dried potato shreds and crumbled meat or bacon bar in water. Drain and cook with dried onion, parsley, and pepper flakes until browned; then stir in cubed cheese and heat until melted. Serve.

Breakfast Tortillas

Serves: 10 people

Method: skillet

Approximate time: 20 minutes

  2 tablespoons oil or margarine

  1 dozen eggs

  1 onion, diced

  2 tomatos, diced

  1/2 lb. bacon (optional)

  shredded cheese

  2 each tortillas

  sour cream

  salsa

In a skillet add oil or margarine and let it melt. In a bowl add eggs and a little bit of water and scramble. Season to taste. Add eggs mixture and onion and tomato to the skillet. Bacon can be done ahead of time and added at the end. Cook until eggs are firm and all ingredients have been thoroughly cooked. Cheese can be melted on top of the mixture or added later. Place scrambled mix on tortilla; add cheese, salsa, and sour cream if desired. Wrap tortilla and eat.

Spanish Rice with Meatballs

Serves: 4 people

Method: kettle

Approximate time: 30 minutes

Cook 10 minutes in 3 to 4 cups water:

  1 cup dried tomato flakes or several home-dried slices

  2 tablespoons dried onion flakes

  salt and pepper

  freeze-dried or canned meatballs

Add 1 cup quick rice and cook, covered, 8 minutes. If dried meatballs were used, add 1 package gravy mix and cook 1 minute. Serve.

Shrimp Creole

Serves: 4 people

Method: kettle

Approximate time: 30 minutes

Cook 6 minutes in 4 cups water:

> 1/4 cup dried tomatoes
>
> 1/4 cup green pepper flakes
>
> 1 cup quick rice
>
> salt and pepper to taste

Add:

> 1 can shrimp (if dried, cook with above)
>
> 1 package powdered cream of mushroom soup mix; add more water if needed

Heat through. Serve.

Tin Foil Dinners

Serves: 10 to 12 people

Method: open-fire cooking

Approximate time: 35 minutes

> potato for each member of the group
>
> hamburger patty for each member of the group
>
> 4 onions
>
> carrots — 1 per person
>
> cheese — 1 slice per person
>
> salt and pepper to taste

Dice the potato, onion, and carrot. On a sheet of aluminum foil, have each participant put potato, ground beef (if used), carrots, onion, and cheese. Salt and pepper to taste. Fold the aluminum foil so that ingredients or juices do not leak out. Place on a bed of coals and let cook until all vegetables and meat are thoroughly cooked.

Variation

Instead of using ground beef, use an additional half potato for each member.

Angels on Horseback

Serves: 10 to 12 people

Method: skillet or grill

Approximate time: 15 minutes

hotdogs

cheese

buns

Slit the hotdog down the middle. Add cheese and either place in a skillet or on a stick to be roasted over an open fire. Be sure to cook the hotdogs with the cheese side up. Hint: If using a skillet, place a lid over the top so it cooks more evenly and quickly. Serve on buns and add seasoning individually to taste.

Desserts

Banana Boats

Serves: 10 people

Method: open fire

Approximate time: 15 minutes

banana (1 per participant)

mini-marshmallows

chocolate chips

aluminum foil

Using your knife, begin by cutting a small strip of banana skin, about a half inch wide, leaving one end of the skin attached to the rest of the skin. Core out part of the banana, creating a boat. In the hollowed-out area, place chocolate chips and marshmallows. Cover with the skin and wrap in aluminum foil. Place over hot coals and allow to bake until chocolate and marshmallows are melted. Serve warm.

S'mores

Serves: as many as you have ingredients for

Method: open fire

Approximate time: 1 – 2 minutes

marshmallows

graham crackers

chocolate bar (1 per person)

Place marshmallow on skewer or stick and roast over fire. When cooked to satisfaction, place on graham cracker with chocolate bar (to fit cracker) and top with another graham cracker and eat.

Baked Apple

Serves: 10 people

Method: open fire

Approximate time: 20 minutes

apple (1 per person)

brown sugar

butter

cinnamon

marshmallows

aluminum foil

Core the apple and fill with brown sugar, butter, cinnamon, and marshmallow. Be sure that the marshmallow is at the top to plug the hole. Wrap in aluminum foil and place on coals or in a covered pot. Remove when tender and eat.

Trip Planning Template

Outdoor
Living
Skills™

Leader:		
Location:		
Date of Trip:		
Duration of Trip (days or hours):		
# Participants:		Age Range:
Adults Attending:	Phone Number	e-mail address

Participant Name	Age	Medical Release	Orientation	Swim y/n	Emergency Contact/Phone #

Outdoor
Living
Skills™

Lodging	
• Where are you staying?	
• How much will it cost (per night, total)?	
• How many sites or rooms will you need?	
• How many nights do you need to reserve?	
Transportation	
• How will you get there?	
• Estimated cost for vehicle?	
• Who's driving?	
• Will you need additional transportation once on site?	
• Estimated cost for gas?	
• How are you paying for gas? (credit card or cash)	
Food	
• How many meals will you have?	
Breakfast? _____ Lunch? _____ Dinner? _____ Snacks? _____	
• How are you going to store it while travelling and onsite?	
• What equipment will you need to prepare, eat and clean up from meals?	
• Who's shopping for supplies?	
• Estimated cost for food supplies	

Outdoor
Living
Skills™

Recreation	
• What recreational activities (hiking, climbing, rafting…) will you be doing?	
• Is there an additional cost?	
• Do participants need to bring additional equipment?	
Group Equipment	
• What kind of equipment will the group need to bring (cooking equipment, utensils, camp kits, tents, packs, stoves etc.)	
• Where are you going to get it?	
• Who is responsible for bringing it to the site?	
Individual Equipment	
• What kind of equipment does each person needs to bring?	
• What specialized equipment do they need to bring specific to the project (bug spray, hats, glove…)	
Budget	
• What is your budget for the total cost of the trip (include cost of trans., lodging, meals, equipment rental, recreation misc expenses etc)	
• What will you charge each participant to attend? Take into account any fundraising that might help offset costs to participants	

Outdoor
Living
Skills™

Responsibilities	
• Do you have a list of daily responsibilities and who is assigned to each task? Remember to include cooking, dishwashing, equipment maintenance, packing and food preparation, establishing a safety monitor etc.	
Risk Management	
• What are your procedures for safety and emergency situations?	
• Does your sponsoring agency already have emergency procedures in place? What are they?	
• Do you have liability releases or waivers and permission forms for participants to sign?	
• What insurance coverage do you need to have for this project and who is responsible for insurance (participants, sponsoring agency, land agency)	
• Do you have emergency contact numbers for all participants?	
• Do you have health forms and emergency permission to treat forms for all participants including adults?	
• What first aid equipment will you need on this trip? One big kit, small kits for breakout groups?	
• Who is certified in first aid and CPR?	

OLS Level Requirements

Level I - Earth

- Plan and go on a hike with a snack

- Describe the buddy system and why you use it with any outdoor activity

- Discuss procedures for staying found

- Name the ten essentials you should have on every trip

- List and discuss safety rules for hiking

- Explain the importance of drinking water

- Identify where you go and what to do if you are sick or injured

- Identify natural outdoor hazards and ways to avoid them

- Identify and draw pictures of poisonous or harmful plants

- Identify where to go to the bathroom on a day hike

- Explain why the group needs a first aid kit

- Play a nature game that helps you understand ecology

- Using your senses of sight, touch, smell, and hearing, describe ten things in your outdoor or camping area

- Describe what minimum impact means

- Draw picture or make poster showing animals, birds, and insects in their natural environment and explain how to watch, protect and respect them

- Describe what makes good outdoor food

- Plan and prepare a snack for a hike

- Describe different methods (heat sources) for cooking

- Plan and prepare a lunch

- Clean up the site after lunch

- Explain what to do with garbage from your hike

- Demonstrate the proper use and storage of a peeler and can opener

- Demonstrate two stopper knots: an overhand and a figure eight knot

- Describe what these knots are used for

- Describe and show the different parts of a rope used for knot tying

- Show how to hold a compass, demonstrate how to find north, south, east, and west

- Describe what can prevent a compass from working properly

- Locate your home or camp on a highway or city map

- Draw a simple map of your camp or neighborhood

Level II - Sun

- Plan and go on an all-day hike with a lunch meal that doesn't require cooking

- Pack a day pack

- Discuss appropriate clothing for your hike

- Describe different kinds of shelters and what situations to use them in

- Demonstrate how to set up a tarp tent or emergency shelter

- Discuss personal health practices in camp

- Describe your water source for the hike

- Identify three plants, animals, and insects that are harmful to humans

- Name three things that might require first aid

- Explain what to do if you see a wild animal such as a bear

- Describe steps to take in the event of a thunderstorm

- Recite the OLS pledge

- Describe what it means to pollute and identify three places that are polluted and why

- Describe what you can do to minimize pollution

- Describe the LAWS of nature

- While camping or hiking, identify camouflaged animals and birds

- Describe two animals that use adaptations in their environment

- Describe where to build an open fire and when it is appropriate

- Identify and find tinder, kindling, and small fuel

- Demonstrate how to build a fire

- Demonstrate appropriate methods for extinguishing a fire and discuss appropriate methods for disposing of the remaining contents and why you would do so

- Plan, prepare, and cook one meal and one snack

- Demonstrate the safe and proper use of a trowel and paring knife

- Demonstrate two joiner knots: a square knot and a sheet bend

- Describe what these knots are used for

- Explain the difference between a planimetric map and topographical map and how each is used

- Demonstrate how to find the cardinal points and inner cardinal points on a compass

- Determine the average length of your pace

- Measure 150 feet by pacing

Level III - Water

- Plan and go on an overnight trip with three meals

- Pack an overnight backpack

- Demonstrate how to properly fit a backpack

- Describe the criteria for selecting a tent site

- Demonstrate how to set up a tent

- Describe the proper way to layer your clothing and why it is important

- List and discuss safety rules for an overnight trip

- Explain how to prevent injuries from happening

- Identify contents of first aid kit and for what contents are used

- Describe two different toilet practices and when you should use them

- Identify the signs of serious weather conditions in your area and what you should do

- Describe a consumer and a producer and why they are important

- Create a model of the water cycle with your leader and describe the process
- Describe what an ecosystem is
- Identify evidence of people in the area and make a list of things people can do to reduce impact on the environment
- Describe two different cloud types and the weather that is associated with them
- Describe safety precautions for using a camp stove
- With appropriate adult supervision, demonstrate proper use of a camp stove
- Plan and carry out sanitization of cooking utensils, dishes, trash, etc.
- Demonstrate methods of care, storage and protection of food from insects, animals, and spoilage
- Plan three meals, cooking at least two
- Demonstrate the safe and proper use of a pocket knife
- Demonstrate the safe and proper way to sharpen a knife
- Explain the difference between a knot and a hitch
- Demonstrate a clove hitch and a half hitch
- Learn about the Big Dipper and use it to find the north star
- Identify north, the legend, and three landmarks on a topographic map
- With a group, lay a compass course using five changes of direction, identifying bearings and distance at each change
- Follow a compass course another group has set

Level IV - Weather

- Plan a two-night overnight with a complete menu for five meals with three away from base camp
- Go on overnight trip with a group using tent or tarp shelter
- Plan the cooking gear needed
- Pack your personal gear and help pack the group gear for your trip
- Develop and sign an individual health and safety agreement
- Discuss and know your responsibilities for first aid

- Help prepare a group first aid kit
- Demonstrate at least one method for purifying water and describe one other method
- Learn effects of cold, and heat, related illnesses and what to do if you encounter them
- Discuss the relationship of plants and animals in the ecosystem
- Define an omnivore, herbivore, and carnivore and give an example of each
- Observing clouds, wind, and temperature, predict the weather daily for a week
- Discuss the weather conditions for your trip
- Demonstrate how to hang your food to protect it
- Describe at least two other ways to protect your food on trail
- Prepare one meal without cooking
- Help plan and pack the food for the trip
- Identify tools needed for overnight
- Demonstrate their use, care, safety, and storage
- Discuss type, size, use, and care of ropes in camp
- Demonstrate how to tie a bowline and a taughtline hitch
- Make a simple map of an outdoor area using a compass and pacing
- Describe what declination is, and how and why we need to adjust for declination
- Describe how you can determine direction without a compass

Level V - Stars

- Write a trip plan for a three-night overnight with non-motorized travel
- Write an emergency plan for your trip and include a communications plan, and file it with the appropriate people
- Assist in leading the planned trip with appropriate adult supervision
- Assist a younger group in properly fitting their pack
- Take a basic community first aid course
- Evaluate safety rules for a three-night trip

- Have your group sign a health and safety agreement, and discuss why it is necessary

- Learn common health or allergy problems of your group

- Carry out a sanitation plan having minimum impact on the environment

- Participate in a conservation project for at least one day and write a newsletter article, story, or poem on the experience

- Describe the food chain and how humans fit into the chain

- Keep a journal of your weather predictions and the actual weather

- Plan complete menus considering nutritional needs, demands of the activity, availability of water, type of food needed for safe consumption, and minimum impact on the environment

- Pack food for the trip and work with the group to decide on meal responsibilities during the trip

- Explain why saws, axes, and other cutting tools are not appropriate for use in minimum impact programs

- Demonstrate whipping a rope

- Teach how to tie a stopper knot, a joiner knot, and a hitch

- Plan an off-trail hike in an appropriate area using a map and compass

- Use a topographical map to route your trip and identify areas where the route may be more difficult

- Teach a group to use a compass course

- During your trip, identify your landmark and take a bearing at least three times

OLS Levels Grid

Skills	Level 1 – Earth	Level 2 – Sun	Level 3 – Water	Level 4 – Weather	Level 5 – Stars
On Your Way	Plan and go on a hike with a snack	Plan and go on an all day hike with a lunch meal that doesn't require cooking	Plan and go on an overnight trip with 3 meals	Plan a 2-night overnight with a complete menu for 5 meals with 3 away from base camp	Write a trip plan for a 3 night overnight with non-motorized travel
	Describe the buddy system and why you use it with any outdoor activity	Pack a day pack	Pack an overnight backpack	Go on overnight trip with a group using tent or tarp shelter	Write an emergency plan for your trip and include a communications plan and file it with the appropriate people
	Discuss procedures for staying found	Discuss appropriate clothing for your hike	Demonstrate how to properly fit a backpack	Plan the cooking gear needed	Assist in leading the planned trip with appropriate adult supervision
	Name the ten essentials you should have on every trip	Describe different kinds of shelters and what situations to use them in	Describe the criteria for selecting a tent site	Pack your personal gear and help pack the group gear for your trip	Assist a younger group in properly fitting their pack
		Demonstrate how to set up a tarptent or emergency shelter	Demonstrate how to set up a tent		
			Describe the proper way to layer your clothing and why it is important		

Being Safe					
	List and discuss safety rules for hiking	Discuss personal health practices in camp	List and discuss safety rules for an overnight trip	Discuss and know your responsibilities for first aid	Take a basic community first aid course
	Explain the importance of drinking water	Describe your water source for the hike	Explain how to prevent injuries from happening	Help prepare a group first aid kit	Evaluate safety rules for 3 night trip
	Identify where you go and what to do if you are sick or injured	Identify 3 plants, animals and insects that are harmful to humans	Identify contents of first aid kit and for what contents are used	Demonstrate at least one method for purifying water and describe one other method	Have your group sign a health and safety agreement, and discuss why it is necessary
	Identify natural outdoor hazards and ways to avoid them	Name 3 things that might require first aid	Describe 2 different toilet practices and when you should use them	Learn effects of clod and heat related illnesses and what to do if you encounter them	Learn common health or allergy problems of your group
	Identify and draw pictures of poisonous or harmful plants	Explain what to do if you see a wild animal such as a bear	Identify the signs of serious weather conditions in your area and what you should do	Develop and sign an individual health and safety agreement	Carry out a sanitation plan having minimum impact on the environment
	Identify where to go to the bathroom on a day hike	Describe steps to take in the event of a thunderstorm			
	Explain why the group needs a first aid kit				

Exploring Your World					
	Play a nature game that helps you understand ecology Using your senses of sight, touch, smell and hearing describe 10 things in your outdoor or camping area Describe what minimum impact means Draw picture or make poster showing animals, birds, insects in their natural environment and explain how to watch, protect and respect them.	Recite the OLS pledge Describe what it means to pollute and identify three places that are polluted and why Describe what you can do to minimize pollution Describe the LAWS of nature While camping or hiking, identify camouflaged animals and birds Describe two animals that use adaptations in their environment	Describe a consumer and a producer and why they are important Create a model of the water cycle with your leader and describe the process Describe what the food chain is and where we fit into it Identify evidence of people in the area and make a list of things people can do to reduce impact on the environment. Describe two different cloud types and the weather that is associated with them	Draw an example of an ecosystem Define an omnivore, herbivore and carnivore and give an example of each Observing clouds, wind & temperature, predict the weather daily for a week Discuss the weather conditions for your trip	Participate in a conservation project for at least one day and write a newsletter article, story or poem on the experience Describe the food chain & how humans fit into the chain Keep a journal of the your weather predictions & the actual weather

Putting It On Your Plate					
	Describe what makes good outdoor food Plan and prepare a snack for a hike Describe different methods (heat sources) for cooking Plan and prepare a lunch Clean up the site after lunch Explain what to do with garbage from your hike	Describe where to build an open fire and when it is appropriate Identify and find tinder, kindling, and small fuel Demonstrate how to build a fire Demonstrate appropriate methods for extinguishing a fire and discuss appropriate methods for disposing of the remaining contents and why you would do so Plan, prepare and cook one meal and one snack	Describe safety precautions for using a camp stove With appropriate adult supervision demonstrate proper use of a camp stove Plan and carry out sanitization of cooking utensils, dishes, trash etc Demonstrate methods of care, storage and protection of food from insects, animals and spoilage Plan 3 meals, cooking at least 2	Demonstrate how to hang your food to protect it Describe at least 2 other ways to protect your food on trail Prepare one meal without cooking Help plan and pack the food for the trip	Plan complete menus considering nutritional needs, demands of the activity, availability of water, type of food needed for safe consumption & minimum impact on the environment Pack food for the trip and work with the group to decide on meal responsibilities during the trip

Tools and Ties				
Demonstrate the proper use and storage of a peeler and can opener	Demonstrate the safe and proper use of a trowel and paring knife	Demonstrate the safe and proper use of a pocket knife	Identify tools needed for overnight	Explain why saws, axes and other cutting tools are not appropriate for use in minimum impact programs
Demonstrate two stopper knots: an overhand and a figure eight knot	Demonstrate 2 joiner knots: a square knot and a sheet bend	Demonstrate the safe and proper way to sharpen a knife	Demonstrate their use, care, safety and storage	Demonstrate whipping a rope
Describe what these knots are used for	Describe what these knots are used for	Explain the difference between a knot and a hitch	Discuss type, size, use & care of ropes in camp	Teach how to tie a stopper knot, a joiner knot and a hitch
Describe and show the different parts of a rope used for knot tying		Demonstrate a clove hitch and a half hitch	Demonstrate how to tie a bowline and a taughtline hitch	

Finding Your Way				
Show how to hold a compass, demonstrate how to find north, south, east and west Describe what can prevent a compass from working properly Locate your home or camp on a highway or city map Draw a simple map of your camp or neighborhood	Explain the difference between a planimeteric map and topographical map and how each is used Demonstrate where the cardinal points and inner cardinal points are on a compass Determine the average length of your pace Measure 150 feet by pacing	Identify north, the legend and 3 landmarks on a topographic map Demonstrate how to take a bearing and how to find a bearing With a group, lay a compass course using 5 changes of direction, identifying bearings & distance at each change Follow a compass course another group has set	Make a simple map of an outdoor area using a compass and pacing Describe what declination is, how and why we need to adjust for declination Learn about the Big Dipper and use it to find the north star Describe how you can determine direction without a compass	Plan an off trail hike in an appropriate area using a map and compass Use a topographical map to route your trip And identify areas where the route may be more difficult Teach a group to use a compass course During your trip, identify your landmark and take a bearing at least three times

OLS Skills Sheets

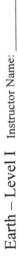

Outdoor Living Skills®

Earth – Level I   Instructor Name: _____   Session _____   Year _____

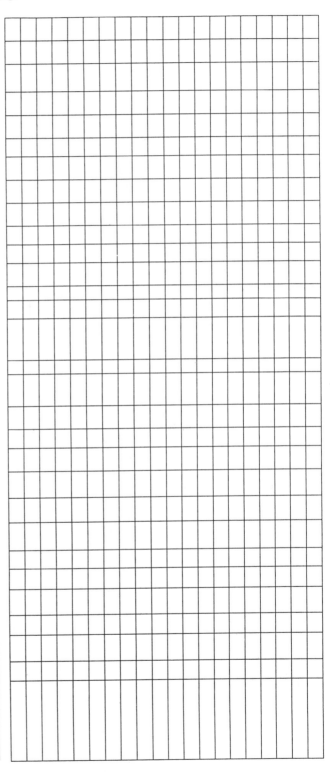

Skills (row labels, top to bottom):

- Draw a simple map of your camp or neighborhood
- Locate your home or camp on a highway or city map
- Describe what can prevent a compass from working properly
- Show how to hold a compass, demonstrate how to find north, south, east and west
- Describe and show the different parts of a rope used for knot tying
- Describe what these knots are used for
- Demonstrate two stopper knots: an overhand and a figure eight knot
- Demonstrate the proper use and storage of a peeler and can opener
- Explain what to do with garbage from your hike
- Clean up the site after lunch
- Plan and prepare a lunch
- Describe different methods (heat sources) for cooking
- Plan and prepare a snack for a hike
- Describe what makes good outdoor food
- Draw picture or make poster showing animals, birds, insects in their natural environment and explain how to watch, protect and respect them.
- Describe what minimum impact means
- Using your senses of sight, touch, smell and hearing describe 10 things in your outdoor or camping area
- Play a nature game that helps you understand ecology
- Explain why the group needs a first aid kit
- Identify where to go to the bathroom on a day hike
- Identify and draw pictures of poisonous or harmful plants
- Identify natural outdoor hazards and ways to avoid them
- Identify where you go and what to do if you are sick or injured
- Explain the importance of drinking water
- List and discuss safety rules for hiking
- Name the ten essentials you should have on every trip
- Discuss procedures for staying found
- Describe the buddy system and why you use it with any outdoor activity
- Plan and go on a hike with a snack

Participant Name

Sun – Level II

Instructor Name: _____ Session _____ Year _____

Outdoor Living Skills®

Participant Name

Skills checklist columns:

- Plan and go on an all day hike with a lunch meal that doesn't require cooking
- Pack a day pack
- Discuss appropriate clothing for your hike
- Describe different kinds of shelters and what situations to use them in
- Demonstrate how to set up a tarptent or emergency shelter
- Discuss personal health practices in camp
- Describe your water source for the hike
- Identify 3 plants, animals and insects that are harmful to humans
- Name 3 things that might require first aid
- Explain what to do if you see a wild animal such as a bear
- Describe steps to take in the event of a thunderstorm
- Recite the OLS pledge
- Describe what it means to pollute and identify three places that are polluted and why
- Describe what you can do to minimize pollution
- Describe the LAWS of nature
- While camping or hiking, identify camouflaged animals and birds
- Describe two animals that use adaptations in their environment
- Describe where to build an open fire and when it is appropriate
- Identify and find tinder, kindling, and small fuel
- Demonstrate how to build a fire
- Demonstrate appropriate methods for extinguishing a fire and discuss appropriate methods for disposing of the remaining contents
- Plan, prepare and cook one meal and one snack
- Demonstrate the safe and proper use of a trowel and paring knife
- Demonstrate 2 joiner knots: a square knot and a sheet bend
- Describe what these knots are used for
- Explain the difference between a planimetric map and topographical map and how each is used
- Demonstrate how to find the cardinal points and inner cardinal points on a compass
- Determine the average length of your pace
- Measure 150 feet by pacing

Outdoor Living Skills® — Water – Level III

Instructor Name: _____ Session _____ Year _____

Participant Name	Plan and go on an overnight trip with 3 meals	Pack an overnight backpack	Demonstrate how to properly fit a backpack	Describe the criteria for selecting a tent site	Demonstrate how to set up a tent	Describe the proper way to layer your clothing and why it is important	List and discuss safety rules for an overnight trip	Explain how to prevent injuries from happening	Identify contents of first aid kit and for what contents are used	Describe 2 different toilet practices and when you should use them	Identify the signs of serious weather conditions in your area and what you should do	Describe a consumer and a producer and why they are important	Create a model of the water cycle with your leader and describe the process	Describe what an ecosystem is	Identify evidence of people in the area and make a list of things people can do to reduce impact on the environment	Describe two different cloud types and the weather that is associated with them	Describe safety precautions for using a camp stove	With appropriate adult supervision demonstrate proper use of a camp stove	Plan and carry out the sanitizing of cooking utensils, dishes, trash etc	Demonstrate methods of care, storage and protection of food from insects, animals and spoilage	Plan 3 meals, cooking at least 2	Demonstrate the safe and proper use of a pocket knife	Demonstrate the safe and proper way to sharpen a knife	Explain the difference between a knot and a hitch	Demonstrate a clove hitch and a half hitch	Learn about the Big Dipper and use it to find the north star	Identify north, the legend and 3 landmarks on a topographic map	With a group, lay a compass course using 5 changes of direction, identifying bearings & distance at each change	Follow a compass course another group has set

Outdoor Living Skills® — Weather – Level IV

Instructor Name: _____   Session _____   Year _____

Participant Name	Plan a 2-night overnight with a complete menu for 5 meals with 3 away from base camp	Go on an overnight trip with a group using tent or tarp shelter	Plan the cooking gear needed	Pack your personal gear and help pack the group gear for your trip	Develop and sign an individual health and safety agreement	Discuss and know your responsibilities for first aid	Help prepare a group first aid kit	Demonstrate at least one method for purifying water and describe one other method	Learn effects of cold and heat related illnesses and what to do if you encounter them	Discuss the relationship of plants & animals in the ecosystem	Define an omnivore, herbivore and carnivore and give an example of each	Observing clouds, wind & temperature, predict the weather daily for a week	Discuss the weather conditions for your trip	Demonstrate how to hang your food to protect it	Describe at least 2 other ways to protect your food on trail	Prepare one meal without cooking	Help plan and pack the food for the trip	Identify tools needed for overnight	Demonstrate their use, care, safety and storage	Discuss type, size, use & care of ropes in camp	Demonstrate how to tie a bowline and a taughtline hitch	Make a simple map of an outdoor area using a compass and pacing	Describe what declination is, how and why we need to adjust for declination	Describe how you can determine direction without a compass

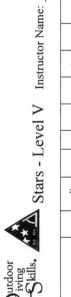

Qutdoor Living Skills. ▲ Stars - Level V   Instructor Name: _____   Session _____   Year _____

Participant Name	Write a trip plan for a 3 night overnight with non-motorized travel	Write an emergency plan for your trip and include a communications plan and file it with the appropriate people	Assist in leading the planned trip with appropriate adult supervision	Assist a younger group in properly fitting their pack	Take a basic community first aid course	Evaluate safety rules for 3 night trip	Have your group sign a health and safety agreement, and discuss why it is necessary	Learn common health or allergy problems of your group	Carry out a sanitation plan having minimum impact on the environment	Participate in a conservation project for at least one day and write a newsletter article, story or poem on the experience	Describe the food chain & how humans fit into the chain	Keep a journal of the your weather predictions & the actual weather	Plan complete menus considering nutritional needs, demands of the activity, availability of water, type of food needed for safe consumption & minimum	Pack food for the trip and work with the group to decide on meal responsibilities during the trip	Explain why saws, axes and other cutting tools are not appropriate for use in minimum impact programs	Demonstrate whipping a rope	Teach how to tie a stopper knot, a joiner knot and a hitch	Plan an off trail hike in an appropriate area using a map and compass	Use a topographical map to route your trip	And identify areas where the route may be more difficult	Teach a group to use a compass course	During your trip, identify your landmark and take a bearing at least three times	Comments

am Manual

MI-SPI

DATE DUE

JUL 0 7 2003			
Res 8/2003			
HP 2d Etienne			
DEC 1 6 2011			

Demco, Inc. 38-293